UNDERSTANDING SOCCER HOOLIGANISM

John H. Kerr

Open University Press
Buckingham · Philadelphia

Open University Press
Celtic Court
22 Ballmoor
Buckingham
MK18 1XW

and

1900 Frost Road, Suite 101
Bristol, PA 19007, USA

First Published 1994

A catalogue record of this book is available from the British Library

ISBN 0 335 19249 1 (pb)   0 335 19250 5 (hb)

A Library of Congress Cataloging-in-Publication
Number is available for this book

Typeset by Graphicraft Typesetters Ltd., Hong Kong
Printed in Great Britain by Biddles Limited, Guildford and Kings Lynn

To Ken and Vera Smith

CONTENTS

PREFACE

For anyone who has even a passing interest in watching soccer, the events of 29 May 1985 remain etched in the memory forever. This was the date of the 1985 European Cup final between Liverpool and Juventus, played in Belgium, at the Heysel Stadium in Brussels. I was late getting away from work and I rushed home to watch the game. When I switched on the television, the first pictures I saw were of Juventus fans attacking police and Liverpool fans. My first impression was that Juventus fans were showing us they could be just as good or bad as English soccer hooligans.

Perhaps I should explain that I was watching the game on a Dutch television channel, so my first impression of what was happening was not helped by the football commentator speaking in Dutch, my lack of understanding of Dutch at that time contributing to my lack of true comprehension. Later, I was to realize the true seriousness of events: thirty-nine people lost their lives and many more were seriously injured. What I also did not realize at the time, owing to my late arrival, but that later became apparent, was that the tragedy came about as a result of Liverpool hooligans 'charging' the Juventus supporters.

Some four years later, in April 1989, I sat down in that same Amsterdam flat to find out the football results on the BBC's *Grandstand* transmission. By then I had access to the BBC channels, which could be picked up in Amsterdam via cable television. This time I was early but, suddenly, scheduled programmes were interrupted and a sombre commentator said we were going over live to Hillsborough in Sheffield, to the Liverpool versus Nottingham Forest FA Cup semi-final, which was not being shown until that evening. Naturally, like many others in Britain and Europe, I sat glued to the TV screen for the rest of the night as, once again, a series of staggering events unfolded. Ironically, that afternoon, the BBC was also showing the World Snooker Championships at Sheffield's Crucible Theatre, not far from the soccer stadium. For a period the broadcast took on a bizarre nature, switching back and forth from the relative calm of the snooker table to the chaotic horror at Hillsborough. I watched, totally engrossed, not believing the pictures of horror that I was seeing. Eventually, it became obvious to those at the game and to viewers at home that another terrible football tragedy was taking place. A late rush of spectators had run into an already full enclosure of Liverpool fans, causing a desperate crush.

The next day, from a special Sunday morning edition of *Breakfast Time*, the BBC's weekday morning news programme, and the articles in the *Observer* newspaper that I had collected from my local Amsterdam newsagent, I learned that over eighty football fans were crushed to death and over 200 others injured. The final figure would turn out to be ninety-five dead. I telephoned my friend and colleague Maurice Punch, a sociologist who has been interested in and had previously written on the subject of soccer hooliganism. I asked if he had heard the news and we talked for some time. We agreed to meet at his house in the afternoon. As we walked around the lake near his home, we discussed the events that had taken place during the previous day in Sheffield.

That day two Dutch soccer teams, Ajax and Feyenoord, were playing a match in Amsterdam. Although it is not as prevalent in Holland as in England, soccer hooliganism is certainly not unknown, and during the previous two days I had noticed the extensive pre-match preparations by the authorities and police. My normal route home from Maurice's house took me past the Olympic Stadium where Ajax play. As I glanced at my watch I knew the match had finished, but thinking that there might be traffic congestion, I decided to take a different route past the Free University. As I pulled up at a red traffic light beside the main university building, a group of about forty youths, obviously football fans, ran out of the bushes and, passing on either side of my car, ran off into an area of housing. The fans, who seemed very young, were not being violent but had cans of beer and were chanting and swearing. I suddenly realized why they were running. Police vans screeched to a halt across the road and policemen piled out. They were wearing full riot gear, helmets with visors and neck protectors, knee and shin protectors, and all carried what looked like American police night sticks (a much longer version of the British policeman's truncheon). All the police chased the supporters, including the dog-handlers, who fought to keep up with the dogs, which, although on leashes, struggled in pursuit. Just as quickly as it had begun, the incident was over: the fans had gone, the police had followed them, the light turned green and I drove off. As a 'hooligan' incident, what I had just experienced hardly rated at all. Doubtless influenced by the events at Hillsborough and Heysel, I think it was at this moment that I made the decision to write the book on soccer hooliganism that I had been contemplating for a couple of years.

Early in 1983 I became interested in what was, at that time, a new theory in psychology, called reversal theory. I had been looking for a

theory that would help to explain motivational factors in sports performance. Reversal theory seemed to offer much better explanations of human
behaviour than other theories I had come across and, more important to
me, explanations that could be applied to sport. I travelled to Cardiff to
meet Mike Apter and we discussed many aspects of reversal theory and its
application to sport. I travelled back to Wales that summer, to take part
in the First International Symposium on Reversal Theory. By 1989, reversal theory had become a major focus of my academic work in sports
psychology and, as I drove home on that Sunday in April 1989, I was
convinced that the theory could also provide an innovative psychological
explanation of why soccer hooliganism takes place.

Although some observers have tried to argue otherwise, soccer hooliganism appears to be a peculiarly English pastime. There have, of course been
domestic soccer hooligan incidents in most Western European countries
and a few incidents have been reported in Eastern European countries.
Where soccer hooliganism does occur in countries like Holland (Punch
1982; Van der Brug and Marseille 1983) and Italy (Roversi 1991), it seems
merely to imitate what has gone on in England over the past thirty years,
and it is a good deal less frequent and much less widespread. Even in other
countries of the British Isles, fighting, when it does occur at soccer games,
is somehow different from the English variety. For example, in Scotland
and Northern Ireland when violence takes place it tends to be based on the
sectarian divisions in those countries (see Murray 1984; Bairner and Sugden
1986; Melnick 1986). Apart from England, few European countries, if any,
have the problem of large numbers of violent hooligans travelling abroad
in search of confrontation with home team hooligans and supporters.

Due to the fact that hooliganism developed in England earlier and on a
larger scale than in other countries, there has been much more written
about the phenomenon by academics, journalists and others. Most of this
material is in English and is written about English hooligans. Although this
book tries to address soccer hooliganism in the widest sense, it unavoid-
ably relies heavily on material that focuses on English soccer hooliganism.

No apology is made for using information from any available source,
including press and television reports (where they are thought to be reliable), academic writing that attempts to provide theoretical explanations
of soccer hooliganism and books and articles written by the soccer fans
and hooligans themselves. Where possible, the results of academic research
are included, but there are a number of problems associated with gathering
empirical evidence on soccer hooligans (e.g. Ingram 1985). The very context in which acts of soccer hooliganism take place means that the collection of quantitative data (for example, using psychological questionnaires)
is extremely difficult, if not impossible. An important means of testing
theoretical hypotheses is thus immediately ruled out. Second, participant
observation has been utilized, but may be criticized for its subjective nature. Other sources of evidence, such as retrospective film analysis and
interviews with hooligans, are also of questionable value for reasons of

possible bias or expectation effects. In spite of these difficulties, there is enough communality in the results of these different research techniques to provide substantive additional evidence in support of the reversal theory approach.

At this stage, it is important to point out that in this book a distinction is made between fans, supporters and hooligans. Fans and supporters are those people who attend soccer matches purely for the enjoyment of watching the game. Soccer hooligans are those people who go to soccer matches to engage in aggressive and violent behaviour before, during or after the game. However, some of the material in this book contains quotes from other writers and from soccer hooligans themselves. In these quotes the word 'fan' or 'supporter' is used in situations which clearly involve hooligan acts.

Many of the established psychological theories are not versatile enough to provide a real insight into aspects of individual and group psychology involved in soccer hooliganism. Reversal theory, with its adaptable conceptual framework, is able to fill the gap and permit a comprehensive understanding of why soccer hooligans behave in the way they do.

References

Bairner, A. and Sugden, J. (1986). 'Observe the sons of Ulster: football and politics in Northern Ireland', in A. Tomlinson and G. Whannel (eds) *Off the Ball.* London: Pluto Press.

Ingram, R. (1985). 'The psychology of the crowd – a social psychological analysis of British football "hooliganism"'. *Medicine, Science and the Law,* **25**(1), 53–8.

Melnick, M. J. (1986). 'The mythology of football hooliganism: a closer look at the British experience'. *International Review for Sociology of Sport,* **21**(1), 1–19.

Murray, B. (1984). *The Old Firm: Sectarianism, Sport and Society in Scotland.* Edinburgh: J. Donald Publishers.

Punch, M. (1982). 'Voetbal en geweld' ('Football and violence'), in R. C. R. Siekmann (ed.) *Voetbalvandalisme (Football Hooliganism).* Haarlem: De Vrieseborch, pp. 117–27.

Roversi, A. (1991). 'Football violence in Italy.' *International Review for Sociology of Sport,* **26**(4), 311–331.

Van der Brug, H. H. and Marseille, M. (1983). *Achtergronden van vandalisme bij voetbalwedstrijden (The Background of Hooliganism at Football Matches).* Haarlem: De Vrieseborch.

ACKNOWLEDGEMENTS

I would like to thank Mike Apter, Steve Murgatroyd and Mark McDermott for giving their support to the original book proposal. In addition, I am particularly grateful to Mike Apter and Mieke Mitchell for their ongoing encouragement and critical comments on early drafts of the book chapters. Their recommendations helped me to organise the material in the book and greatly improve the text. I would also like to thank the staff at Open University Press, particularly Jacinta Evans for her enthusiasm and assistance in producing this book. Finally, I would like to express my thanks to staff at the International Institute for Sport and Human Performance at the University of Oregon in Eugene where one chapter was written while I was in residence.

Permission to publish Figure 3.1 from R. S. P. Jones and K. J. Heskin (1988) 'Towards a functional analysis of delinquent behaviour: A pilot study', *Counselling Psychology Quarterly*, 1(1), 35–42, granted by Carfax Publishing Company, Abingdon, Oxfordshire, England.

1

INTRODUCTION

Four days in October 1993[1]

Tuesday 12 October 1993, 2.00 p.m.

Tomorrow, Wednesday, the England soccer team are playing against Holland in the Feyenoord stadium in Rotterdam in a crucial Group 2 World Cup qualifying match. The results of games already played in this group mean that whichever team wins tomorrow goes forward to the World Cup finals in the USA next year. The two teams are closely matched and the game looks like being a tremendous soccer contest.

However, the action has already started 'off the field'. England's 'soccer hooligans' are on the rampage in Europe again; this time in Amsterdam. Last night around fifty drunken hooligans attacked people near the red-light district; thirty were arrested and will be deported; a further eight will appear in court to face assault charges for allegedly kicking and beating a passer-by and threatening others with a knife. Close cooperation has taken place between the Dutch and English police and those troublemakers, travelling among the 5,000 fans expected in Rotterdam for tomorrow's soccer game, have been warned, through the English media, of stiff penalties for causing trouble.

Wednesday 13 October 1993, 9.00 a.m.

England manager Graham Taylor has announced a controversial England team for the match in Rotterdam this evening. Eclipsing this information, the lead story on the BBC Breakfast News programme was the report that 197 England 'fans' were arrested in Amsterdam last night. Of those arrested, eleven will appear before the courts charged with violent offences and the rest will be fined and deported back to England. The vast majority of those arrested did not have tickets for the game and were described as unruly holiday makers bent on violence; not genuine soccer fans. Accompanying these details was the now all too familiar film of wrecked bars and smashed windows, police on horseback and others with dogs breaking up groups of fans, fans being handcuffed and thrown into police vans and the usual claim from interviewed fans that the police had been unnecessarily aggressive and violent.

Police are reported to have 700 officers on duty (500 in riot gear) in Rotterdam in order to try to prevent clashes between English and Dutch soccer hooligans. If the English are the most notorious hooligans in Europe, then the Dutch variety probably come second. Although the Dutch do have their own domestic soccer hooligan problem, trouble rarely occurs outside the country and, generally speaking, happens on a smaller scale than in England. Other steps have been taken to keep the Dutch and English apart, such as declaring the sale of tickets outside the stadium illegal, with threats from the police to arrest ticket touts. The American authorities, including FBI and police officials, are watching events here closely because of the potential problem of dealing with English or Dutch hooligans in the USA next year during the finals of the World Cup tournament.

Everything looks set for an English soccer hooligan classic!

Thursday 14 October 1993, 2.00 p.m.

Violence in Rotterdam began yesterday at about 1.00 p.m. as groups of English and Dutch hooligans fought running battles with each other and the police. Just after lunchtime the Deputy Mayor of Rotterdam invoked an emergency by-law giving the police powers to arrest anyone thought likely to cause trouble. Around 400 were taken into preventative custody during the afternoon and held at a marine barracks in the east of the city. According to reports in the Daily Telegraph *the number rose to 950 by the time the soccer match began. One English fan was shot in the leg by a bullet that, a police spokesman said, was fired from behind a group of Dutch supporters. In the city centre a tennis ball bomb, packed with gunpowder and thrown by a Dutch hooligan, exploded in the midst of a group of about twenty English fans. At least one Dutch supporter was beaten senseless by the English hooligans and other groups threw glasses at each other. Ongoing charges by English hooligans, wearing England soccer scarves and shirts, at their Dutch counterparts and by riot police, who attempted to keep groups of English and Dutch apart, occurred throughout the afternoon.

After an exciting match, but a poor England performance, Holland won 2–0. During the game, only a few minor hooligan incidents took place and police kept almost 5,000 English fans, who did have tickets, in the stadium for an hour after the game to give Dutch fans time to clear the stadium. As a result there was little trouble after the match. Police tactics were successful, as English supporters (most of them without match tickets) *who looked as if they would cause trouble were arrested and held at different points in the city. Police estimated that some 1,800 supporters arrived in Rotterdam without tickets and over 1,000 were arrested in Holland. A group of forty of those arrested were handcuffed together and returned to England by ferry, accompanied by Dutch police. Earlier, those arrested in Amsterdam reputedly paid their fares and were flown back to England in charter planes, accompanied by police.*

The media had turned up in force in Rotterdam to record the trouble-makers. The BBC and Dutch news programmes on Wednesday showed film clips of the day's hooligan activity and the British Prime Minister condemning what had occurred. Later that night, at 10.30 p.m., the BBC Newsnight programme had a number of experts available to give their opinions of what should be done about the problems. One academic, who has spent some years studying soccer hooliganism, without specifying details, argued for educational measures in schools that would wean hooligans away from this kind of behaviour. Most of those who had featured in the earlier film coverage from Rotterdam looked to be well past school age. A former England international soccer player contradicted himself when he talked about the 'moronic few' and 'moronic idiots' and then later claimed that the hooligans were intelligent enough to play the innocent one minute, and then suddenly strike when the opportunity arose. By Thursday night, on BBC's Question Time, politicians and others were blaming the Dutch authorities for not prosecuting more of those hooligans they had arrested.

Friday 15 October 1993, 9.00 a.m.

All the British newspapers carried stories with details of British Prime Minister John Major's apology to his Dutch counterpart, Ruud Lubbers, and of the first five hooligans who faced the courts in Rotterdam. A 30-year-old hooligan, said to have attacked a uniformed police officer from behind, causing blood to pour from his ear, received three weeks in prison. The other four, aged 23, 35 and 31 respectively, received suspended prison sentences and fines of £250 or £500. One of this group was convicted of attacking two police officers three minutes after arriving in Rotterdam in a train. The fifth supporter was acquitted. All of those convicted vigorously denied being involved in the violence, but the assistant chief constable of Greater Manchester, who had liaised with Dutch police, was quoted in the Guardian as saying that 'some of the violence in the Netherlands was the worst he had seen'. A further eighteen supporters were spot-fined from £30 to £1,000 in Rotterdam. Nineteen English hooligans, facing charges relating to violent offences, are still under arrest in Amsterdam and seven Dutch fans arrested in Rotterdam go to court in January faced with public order charges.

Calls for tighter government measures to combat soccer hooliganism, which have now become commonplace after England matches abroad, were also to be found in most press reports. The Guardian *reported concern in the Dutch press that the way in which the Rotterdam police had used special powers (invoked by the Deputy Mayor's emergency by-law) to take groups of English supporters into custody was a breach of the rights of the individual and had raised a serious constitutional problem. The Dutch newspaper* Trouw, *for example, was critical of police tactics and quoted one chief constable, from Leiden, who accused the Amsterdam and Rotterdam police of using Eastern bloc methods against innocent citizens. While there was some concern about police methods, the general feeling was that they prevented much worse trouble.*

What has become clear is that the English soccer team, because of this defeat in Holland, now has only a very slim chance of going to the USA for the World Cup finals in 1994. The American authorities have already begun to breathe a sigh of relief – they will probably not have to deal with the English soccer hooligan problem after all.

The soccer hooligan formula does not seem to have changed very much over the years. The description of the events that occurred in Holland in October 1993 could equally well have been written about almost any one of a host of previous domestic or international hooligan incidents. Apart from the larger than ever numbers of supporters taken into custody, with minor changes the description would fit earlier incidents almost perfectly. By way of example, at the European Championship in Germany in 1988, Vuillamy (1988) wrote:

> The worst fighting so far in the European Football Championship broke out last night at Dusseldorf railway station and in the surrounding streets. Tear gas and flares were fired and the police baton-charged the mobs of fans as they fought running battles inside the station forecourt and in the streets opposite. More than 100 arrests were made . . . Some 500 English supporters then chased the Germans and Dutch up the side streets; they were driven back by the police. The police refused to confirm or deny whether the flares and gas were fired by the police or German fans. The rival mobs threw sticks and rocks at each other and some were slightly injured, a few by police truncheons. Police reinforcements streamed into the area. After a number of charges and counter-charges, the crowds were dispersed.

In spite of the fact that soccer hooliganism has been a recurrent problem since at least the 1960s, there have been few satisfactory suggestions made, especially by those charged with dealing with the problem, as to why English soccer hooligans continue to engage in their hooligan behaviour and what effective measures could be taken to try to deal with the problem in the future.

This chapter will attempt to describe and define soccer hooliganism and review some of the important related issues that have become apparent over the past twenty-five or thirty years. A number of theoretical positions, some sociological, some psychological, will be discussed. The idea is not to become embroiled in the theoretical arguments of particular approaches, or to make judgements of which theoretical stance or research is superior to another, but to try to give the flavour of the general line of argument in each case and to pull together relevant and important aspects of work that has already been done. This is difficult to do in a restricted space and thus accounts of others' work may be rather brief. Although some of these pieces of work are now somewhat dated, the arguments made remain largely valid and relevant. It will be shown how these earlier approaches and research results can be accommodated by the eclectic framework of reversal theory (Apter 1982). In Chapter 2, reversal theory will be explained, but before we move on it might be helpful to look at some background information.

What is a soccer hooligan?

The *Oxford Advanced Learner's Dictionary* (Cowie 1989) describes a hooligan as 'a disorderly and noisy young person who often behaves in a violent and destructive way; young thug or ruffian.' The word hooligan has been qualified by the addition of 'soccer' or 'football' because during the last past thirty years the hooligan acts have generally taken place in and around English soccer matches. The words 'in and around' are used because the hooligan acts often have little to do with what is going on during the game and frequently occur outside or well away from the soccer stadium.

Although soccer hooligans do claim allegiance to one soccer team or another, the style of play or success of the team are generally not important. A particular team is merely a kind of 'flag of convenience' that allows the hooligans to pursue their activities against the followers of other teams, the police or members of the public. They differ from the genuine fan or supporter who, like fans in other sports, is passionately interested in soccer, and in one particular team (see Hornby 1992).

Hooligan attacks are usually made against rival hooligan gangs, but hooligan groups, which may well be rivals in England, often unite to form a kind of super hooligan coalition for trips abroad to 'support' the England team (Williams *et al.* 1984). On their return to England after the international match, the temporary union is disbanded and old hooligan rivalries are once again renewed. In spite of hooliganism being regularly associated with club matches in England, hooligan violence at England's home matches is largely unknown.

Destructive and violent behaviour has, on occasion, been associated with American football and some other forms of sport, but these incidents have been much more infrequent and of a different nature to what has become known as soccer hooliganism in England and Europe. A recent article in the American magazine *Sports Illustrated* (Johnson 1993) listed all the major riots that have occurred in North America since 1968, when 200 people were arrested in Detroit after the Tigers baseball team won the World Series. Over the years since 1968, there have been two other incidents of violent celebration in Detroit, but a number of other cities, including Pittsburgh, New York, San Francisco, Montreal, Chicago and Dallas, have all experienced sports-related rioting and vandalism. The trouble has not been limited to any particular sport. As well as baseball, ice hockey, American football and basketball have provoked violence.

The common element in all these events was that the team concerned won the major sports championship in that sport and the resulting destruction, looting and violence seems to have been a spontaneous celebration of victory. For example, in 1993, violent events occurred when the Montreal Canadiens won the Stanley Cup in ice hockey, the Dallas Cowboys won the Superbowl in American football and the Chicago Bulls won the NBA basketball title for the third time. These episodes of violence are what Smith (1983) has called the 'victory celebration' riot. They differ in several respects from English soccer hooliganism, which, for example, is often well planned rather than spontaneous and is not dependent on a team winning for it to occur.

Whereas travelling to away games is relatively easy for English football supporters, the distances involved in travelling to away games in America would seem to militate against large numbers of fans following their team. As a result, the vast majority of fans are home team fans and confrontations between rival fans, of the soccer hooligan type, are less likely to take place. This may be a major reason for the non-development of the English version of sport-related hooliganism in the USA.

Sports hooliganism: not a new occurrence

According to Guttman (1986) there have been problems with sports crowd violence since spectator sports began, before the days of the Greek and Roman empires. As Smith (1983) pointed out, a number of writers claim that riots, not only those in the context of sport, have taken place for reasons of victory and celebration, fun and recreation (e.g. Marx 1972; Beisser 1979; Tilly 1979). In his review, Smith (1983) described a number of different types of sport-related riots. These included: riots that occur as a result of some form of political demonstration; confrontation between rival groups; fans being denied access to an event; a team or an individual's defeat or victory; and, finally, sports events that provide the excuse for the so-called 'time-out' riot. The last of these is likely to occur during special holidays and festivals or, in this case, sports events where deviant and aggressive behaviour, such as drunkenness, fighting and property damage, are widely condoned, by citizens, police and other authorities. In Smith's (1983: 152) opinion:

> Much of what is called soccer hooliganism smacks strongly of time-out behaviour. Most of the scholarly literature on the subject suggests that hooligans are as much motivated by the desire for fun, excitement, and peer status as they are by ethnic, regional, or other animosities. The latter seem a pretext for trouble rather than a cause of it.

Pearson (1983), in his aptly named book *A History of Respectable Fears*, which is a study of street crime and violence in Britain, shows clearly that the idea of soccer hooliganism and other contemporary delinquent behaviour as both recent and escalating in frequency or degree is incorrect. He also presents impressive evidence that hooliganism, rather than being a modern phenomenon, dates back to the seventeenth and eighteenth centuries and even earlier. In doing so, he attacks and explodes the myth of the tranquil, well-ordered stability of the traditional 'British way of life'. In a systematic way, Pearson discounts the reasons given for the alleged upsurge in hooliganism (including increasing irresponsibility of parental care, working mothers, leniency of punishments and the law, educational trends, youths becoming too affluent and the cause of increasing crime figures, and the responsibility of immigrant or outside groups), made prominent by 'every successive wave of concern', 'as nothing more than a litany of hallucinatory fears that bears no relation to reality' (Pearson 1983: 211).

He sees the continuation of these myths in the conflicts between generations and between social classes, and in the seemingly unending tendency to look back nostalgically and be anxious about the future. However, in emphasizing that crime and violence are not new, Pearson states:

> The predominant involvement of young men and boys in so much of this hooligan history is another of these 'raw materials', providing evidence of the biological characteristics of youthfulness as well as possible indications of male aggressiveness and persisting cultural definitions of manliness and machismo. Across the centuries we have seen the same rituals of territorial dominance, trials of strength, gang fights, mockery against elders and authorities, and antagonism towards 'outsiders' as typical focuses for youthful energy and aggressive mischief. Even under vastly different social conditions there are striking continuities between the violent interruptions to pre-industrial fairs and festivals, and the customary eruptions during modern Bank Holidays or the weekly carnival of misrule at contemporary football games – where the modern football rowdy, with his territorial edginess, mascots, emblems and choral arrangements in the 'rough music' tradition, must seem like a reincarnation of the unruly apprentice, or late Victorian 'Hooligan'.
>
> (Pearson 1983: 211)

The soccer-specific variety

Working class origins?

Dunning *et al.* (1982) have traced the development of soccer hooliganism in England since the late 1800s. From an examination of local and national newspaper reports over the years in detail, they conclude that soccer hooliganism, although not necessarily progressive, has been a feature of soccer crowds for about 100 years. It seems to have declined somewhat until the mid-1960s when, in their opinion, the soccer hooliganism problem became a 'national cause for concern'. Writing in 1984, I. Taylor questions the evidence, presented by Dunning and his colleagues, that violent incidents have occurred throughout soccer's professional history. He does agree, however, that 'there is *no* equivalent period in British soccer history to the 25-year period of more or less continuous soccer hooliganism beginning in 1961' (I. Taylor 1984: 176).

A number of sources of material (e.g. Harrington 1968; Trivizas 1980) are cited by Dunning *et al.* (1982) to support their view that the majority of soccer hooligans are from the lower working class. In their view, the structure of working class communities, in which the 'rough working class tradition' and 'violent masculine style' are inherent features of the social composition, is the structure of soccer hooligan groups. They go on to argue that the way these communities are structured can best be understood in terms of 'ordered segmentation' (see Suttles 1968). Here, in response to threat or conflict, largely independent bigger communities combine together in an ordered way according to a relatively permanent lineage. For example, rival council housing estates may join together at soccer matches to take on the supporters of the visiting team or, as mentioned above, hooligans from different clubs may band together when England are playing abroad, in order to fight with foreign hooligans.

The strong links between soccer and working class people described above have been the focus of other writing (e.g. Taylor 1971, 1982; Clarke, 1978; Corrigan 1979) that has attempted to underline the importance of soccer as a feature of what Taylor (1976) has termed the 'working class weekend'. The 'working class weekend' incorporates the traditional leisure pursuits developed in the second half of the nineteenth century, such as brass bands, archery and whippet racing, that working class males from industrial communities engaged in at the weekend. By the early 1900s, spectating at professional soccer had become a widely popular feature of the English working class weekend.

Taylor (1976) claims that soccer-related violence can be explained by examining the changing opportunities and increasing choice of leisure and sporting activities for young working class males. The development of alternative commercial entertainment, available not only at the weekend but also through the week, has had a significant influence on the weekend leisure activity of the working class. Previously, soccer had formed the focal point of collective adolescent weekend activity. It is the development of a consumer 'culture of style, glamour and excitement' geared to the individual, argues Taylor (1976), that is directly responsible for the 'collapse of the working class weekend'. As a result, soccer-related (and other forms of youth) violence can be seen as attempts by disaffected working class adolescents to re-establish the traditional working class weekend.

For the rough working class, the 'play-fight' nature of a soccer game, with its variety and range of male dominance characteristics, appeals to their masculine values. In addition, another attraction of soccer for the working class is that the excitement generated by attending matches is in direct contrast with the boredom of everyday working life: 'in the communities of the "rough" working class, violence tends to occur to a greater extent in public and to take, on balance, an "expressive" or "affectual" form. As such, it tends to be associated to a greater extent with the arousal of pleasurable feelings' (Dunning *et al.* 1982: 143).

While sociological perspectives on the working class orientation of soccer hooliganism would appear to have a certain level of credibility, there is plenty of more recent evidence to suggest that those involved in hooliganism are not limited to the working class communities (e.g. E. Taylor 1984; Buford 1991). However, the ideas expressed about the boredom of everyday life and the pleasurable arousal associated with hooligan violence are themes that recur throughout this book and are especially relevant to reversal theory (Apter 1982) explanations of soccer hooligan behaviour. There are, however, some other aspects of the soccer environment that may have contributed to the development of soccer hooliganism and that need to be considered before we move on to the details of reversal theory. These are the match environment itself and the manner in which the media have dealt with the reporting of soccer hooligan violence.

The match environment

Canter *et al.* (1989) took environmental psychology as a basis for their study of the social and physical context of soccer. Their approach was concerned with aspects of human behaviour and experience in particular places (e.g. sports stadia) and how, for example, physical surroundings can affect human actions and well-being. Of importance to the authors were the differing perspectives, as a consequence of different types of interaction, that different individuals have about the same place (e.g. spectators and police). In addition, people's perceptions of particular places, the type or status of the people in attendance and what takes place there often colour judgements and beliefs and, as a result, may influence behaviour. Therefore, a priority of the study was to obtain objective data by systematically questioning the various groups involved with the soccer 'place' for their opinions. The results of Canter *et al.*'s (1989) research work indicated a number of common causes for concern. For example, spectators expressed their concern about the general physical conditions encountered at soccer grounds in England. This, however, varied from club to club and the authors point out that each club tends to have its own culture and warn against the dangers of treating soccer supporters as a homogeneous group. The handling of large crowds of people attending matches, especially in emergencies, was found to be inadequate. The authors endorse a trend towards better management, training and effective communication between club authorities, police and fans. Spectators were also found to be concerned about hooligan violence at soccer matches and this is reported as one reason why fewer fans are attending soccer games.

Finally, Canter *et al.* (1989) argue for a change in the way soccer grounds are perceived. They state:

> It is surprisingly rare for football grounds to be discussed in these terms so there is really very little information about how successful football grounds actually are as recreation or entertainment facilities ... We believe that it is essential to think of the recreational experience of football grounds because the experience we have described may be destroyed by the way grounds are designed, managed and policed.
>
> Canter *et al.* 1989: 127)

Soccer hooliganism and the media

One topic that constantly arises in any debate on soccer hooliganism is whether or not coverage by television, radio and the press exacerbates the problem. Most observers (e.g. Hall 1978; Whannel 1979; Williams 1986; Young 1986) agree that the type of publicity given to soccer hooliganism, especially by the press and television, certainly has not been helpful. In this respect, Taylor (1982) pointed out that the general consensus in press and television reporting was that the reformist 'soft' option to the problem should be dropped and that stronger punishment for the individuals concerned should be implemented. It appears that media coverage of this type has had a tendency to make soccer hooligan activities, with their inherently exciting and negativistic characteristics, attractive to a much wider group of disaffected youth, and to reinforce the behaviour of those hooligans involved in the particular incidents at focus. Cohen (1972), in his book entitled *Folk Devils and Moral Panics*, devoted considerable time to this topic and showed how societal reaction to deviance (youth and other subcultures, vandalism, hooliganism), based on information from the media, often serves to increase deviant behaviour. Cohen (1972) used the term 'deviance amplification', suggested by Wilkins (1964), to describe the processes involved. This process was clearly shown to be at work in Cohen's own study of the Mods and Rockers in Britain during the 1960s which, among other things, examined the media's reaction to the various activities of these groups.

Cohen (1972) also pointed out that the very nature of 'news' in newspapers or on radio and television means that the events reported are unusual, certainly not boring and often sensational, or are at least often presented as sensational (see Coulson 1991). This means that the information available is presented, secondhand, in a manner that will attract readers or viewers and may also be subject to political or commercial control of some sort.

The information about deviance in particular is often presented in a stereotypical fashion. The media have a tendency to act as 'agents of moral indignation', often reporting incidents of deviance in a way that can highlight a need to protect established values. Consequently, such coverage may lead to changes (usually for the worse) in the public's perception of events and generate feelings of anxiety or perhaps panic. It may also reinforce the behaviour of the hooligans, by giving the individuals concerned the excitement and pleasure of seeing themselves and their friends in media reports. In addition, others not involved in the particular hooligan incidents being shown or written about may become attracted to, and eventually be drawn into, similar hooligan activities. Consequently, as far as soccer hooliganism is concerned, the media's role may be as an amplifier of deviance, but might also be more accurately described as 'an amplifier of violence'. As Dunning *et al.* (1982: 154), in discussing media coverage in the mid 1960s, emphasized,

> An 'amplification spiral' was set in motion and, in that context, the media resorted increasingly to a rhetoric of violence, frequently exaggerating the level and extent of the violence that was actually involved. Widespread publicity was given to a definition of match days and football grounds as times and places where 'real' fights regularly took place and, as an unintended consequence, football became publicly defined in a manner that made it consonant with the norms and values of violent masculinity. Hence, the attractiveness of the game to adolescent and young adult males, from communities characterized by ordered segmentation, was increased as they started attending matches more regularly and frequently than ever before.

Soccer hooligan violence: an illusion?

Aggro: the Illusion of Violence, a book written by Marsh (1978), brought a different perspective to soccer hooliganism by questioning the reality of hooligan violence. Marsh and his colleagues (1978) used video film, backed up by participant observation and interview material from fans and hooligans, to examine the behaviour of soccer hooligans on the terraces in some detail. Using the approach of Harré and Secord (1972) to analyse their findings, they found that the behaviour of fans followed a set of social rules that tended to govern their ritualistic collective action. The fans and hooligans themselves seemed to be well aware of these rules, and some had particularly important roles to play within the dynamic social interaction on the terraces. The major thrust of Marsh's arguments is that the aggressive and violent behaviour of soccer hooligans is really a ritualistic game. In a nutshell, his approach is captured in the following quotation: '"Aggro" is a way of expressing aggression in a relatively non-injurious manner. Football "hooligans", despite all the mythologies about them which circulate in the media, are currently the most visible exponents in Britain of this ritualistic mode of conflict resolution' (Marsh 1978: 11–12.) For example, when rival groups of soccer hooligans confront each other, the resultant symbolic displays and aggressive threats are designed to make rival supporters back down. Where fighting does occur, the injuries are, generally speaking, not too serious. These episodes, with their own 'rules of engagement' as it were, can be seen as an extension of the play-fight going on between the soccer teams on the field (Dunning *et al.* 1982). According to Marsh (1978) the social rules of soccer hooligan activities are based on traditional values of masculinity, courage and fair play.

If Marsh is correct, in order for this ritualistic confrontation to work effectively in creating excitement and danger, there has to be enough of an element of violence to make it interesting, but not so much that the hooligan game is spoilt. Real violence and serious injury are necessary from time to time to give the game credibility and only occur when the rules are ignored or broken by the 'nutters' or 'hardmen'. Generally speaking, the rules of engagement are thought to act as a constraining factor, maintaining a balance between extremes, and allowing aggression and violence to be experienced within a wider context of relative safety.

Although hundreds of thousands of people attend soccer matches in England every week, on average fewer than five arrests are made by the police (Canter *et al.* 1989: 17) per 10,000 spectators attending soccer matches. Thus, it seems that contrary to media hype, soccer hooligan violence is not as widespread, regular and frequent an aspect of crowd behaviour at soccer matches as some people believe. This is not to say that severe injuries and even deaths do not occur from time to time (see Ward 1989; Buford 1991). As Marsh (1978: 16) points out, 'The contrast is not between total injury and total safety but rather between what would happen if there were no restraints, and what happens in reality.'

Concluding comments

From the summary of the ideas and theories that others have put forward to try to explain soccer hooliganism, it would appear that neither hooliganism in general nor ritualistic aggro are new phenomena. Although some argue that soccer hooliganism also has a long history, others disagree, but most commentators agree that there was an upsurge in soccer hooliganism in the early 1960s. This upsurge may be bound up in the traditions of the rough working class and changes in the pattern of their weekend leisure activity. Other factors, such as the media and the way spectators at soccer matches are treated, may also exaggerate or amplify soccer hooligan behaviour.

In reading and thinking about this material and trying to establish just what kind of problem soccer hooliganism presents, a number of crucial questions come to mind:

1 Are soccer hooligans really moronic idiots or drunken yobs as they are so often portrayed in the media?
2 Is soccer hooliganism a direct result of unemployment and material deprivation?
3 What motivates people to take unnecessary risks, in terms of physical injury or imprisonment, by fighting with rival hooligans or confronting the police?
4 Why do people suddenly become aggressive and violent towards others who have done them no harm?
5 Why are the measures taken by the authorities apparently so ineffective in dealing with soccer hooligans?
6 Why has hooliganism become associated with soccer and not some other sport or activity, and will it continue?
7 Why do some soccer hooligans drop out or move on?

This book will attempt to answer these kinds of questions in a more comprehensive manner than has previously been achieved, by using reversal theory's psychological approach to tackle head on the most crucial and basic question: why do soccer hooligans do what they do? When this question is tackled, answers to the others will also emerge.

Note

1 The factual information presented here was obtained from a number of news-paper articles published in mid-October 1993. Full details of these articles are provided in the reference list under: Connett (1993), Donegan (1993), Fenton and Holden (1993), Goodbody (1993a, b), Kieskamp (1993) and Mullin *et al.* (1993).

References

Apter, M. J. (1982). *The Experience of Motivation: the Theory of Psychological Reversals*. London: Academic Press.

Beisser, A. R. (1979). 'The sports fan and recreational violence'. *Psychiatric Annals*, 9, 78–85.

Buford, B. (1991). *Among the Thugs*. London: Secker & Warburg.

Canter, D., Comber, M. and Uzzell, D. L. (1989). *Football in Its Place*. London: Routledge.

Clarke, J. (1978). 'Football and working class fans: tradition and change', in R. Ingham (ed.) *Football Hooliganism: the Wider Context*. London: Inter-action, pp. 37–60.

Cohen, S. (1972). *Folk Devils and Moral Panics*. Oxford: Basil Blackwell.

Coulson, A. S. (1991). 'Cognitive synergy in televised entertainment', in J. H. Kerr and M. J. Apter (eds) *Adult Play: a Reversal Theory Approach*. Amsterdam: Swets & Zeitlinger, pp. 71–85.

Connett, D. (1993). October 15. 'English football fan jailed for assault on policeman'. *Independent*, 15 October, 5.

Corrigan, P. (1979). *Schooling the Smash Street Kids*. London: Macmillan.

Cowie, A. P. (1989). *Oxford Advanced Learner's Dictionary*. Oxford: Oxford University Press.

Donegan, L. (1993). '600 English fans rounded up'. *Guardian*, 14 October, 1.

Dunning, E., Maguire, J. A., Murphy, P. J. and Williams, J. M. (1982). 'The social roots of football hooliganism'. *Leisure Studies*, 2, 139–56.

Fenton, B. and Holden, W. (1993). '950 held in swoop on soccer hooligans'. *Daily Telegraph*, 14 October, 1.

Goodbody, J. (1993a). 'Dutch to deport 30 football hooligans'. *The Times*, 12 October, 5.

Goodbody, J. (1993b). 'Major promises action to stop football hooligans'. *The Times*, 15 October, 2.

Guttman, A. (1986). *Sports Spectators*. New York: Columbia University Press.

Hall, S. (1978). 'The treatment of "football hooliganism" in the press', in R. Ingham (ed.) *Football Hooliganism: the Wider Context*. London: Inter-action.

Harré, R. and Secord, P. F. (1972). *The Explanation of Social Behaviour*. Oxford: Blackwell.

Harrington, J. A. (1968). *Soccer Hooliganism*. Bristol: John Wright and Sons.

Hornby, N. (1992). *Fever Pitch*. London: Victor Gollancz.

Johnson, W. O. (1993). 'The agony of victory'. *Sports Illustrated*, 5 July, 31–7.

Kieskamp, W. (1993). 'ME'er: Die Engelse supporters hebben recht op excuses' ('Mobile unit member [i.e. riot police]: the English have a right to an apology'). *Trouw*, 15 October, 1.

Marsh, P. (1978). *Aggro: the illusion of Violence*. London: Dent.

Marsh, P., Rosser, E. and Harré, R. (1978). *The Rules of Disorder*. London: Routledge and Kegan Paul.

Marx, G. T. (1972). 'Issueless riots', in J. F. Short and M. E. Wolfgang (eds) *Collective Violence*. Chicago: Aldine-Atherton.

Mullin, J., Donegan, L. and Ward, D. (1993). 'Dutch papers back fans' criticism of police'. *Guardian*, 15 October, 16.

Pearson, G. (1983). *A History of Respectable Fears*. London: Macmillan.

Smith, M. D. (1983). *Violence and Sport*. Toronto: Butterworth.

Suttles, G. D. (1968). *The Social Construction of Communities*. Chicago: University of Chicago Press.

Taylor, E. (1984). 'I was a soccer hooligan – Class of 64'. *Guardian*, 28 March.

Taylor, I. (1971). 'Soccer consciousness and soccer hooliganism', in S. Cohen (ed.) *Images of Deviance*. Harmondsworth: Penguin, pp. 134–64.

Taylor, I. (1976). 'Spectator violence around football: the rise and fall of the "Working Class Weekend"'. *Research Papers in Physical Education*, 4(1), 4–9.

Taylor, I. (1982). 'On the sports violence question: soccer hooliganism revisited', in J. Hargreaves (ed.) *Sport, Culture and Ideology*. London: Routledge and Kegan Paul, pp. 152–96.

Taylor, I. (1984). 'Putting the boot into a working-class sport. British soccer after Bradford and Brussels'. *Sociology of Sport Journal*, 4, 171–91.

Tilly, C. (1979). 'Collective violence in European perspective', in H. D. Graham and T. R. Gurr (eds) *Violence in America: Historical and Comparative Perspectives*. Beverly Hills, CA: Sage.

Trivizas, E. (1980). 'Offences and offenders in football crowd disorders'. *British Journal of Criminology*, **20**(3), 276–88.

Vuillamy, E. (1988). 'Soccer mob hits peak of violence'. *Guardian*, 15 June, 1.

Ward, C. (1989). *Steaming in*. London: Simon and Shuster.

Whannel, G. (1979). 'Football, crowd behaviour and the press'. *Media, Culture and Society*, **1**(4), 327–42.

Wilkins, L. T. (1964). *Social Deviance: Social Policy, Action and Research*. London: Tavistock.

Williams, J. (1986). 'White riots: the English football fan abroad', in A. Tomlinson and G. Whannel (eds) *Off the Ball*. London: Pluto Press, pp. 5–19.

Williams, J., Dunning, E. and Murphy, P. (1986). *Hooligans Abroad*. London: Routledge and Kegan Paul.

Young, K. (1986). '"The killing field": themes in mass media responses to the Heysel Stadium riot'. *International Review for the Sociology of Sport*, **21**, 252–64.

2

REVERSAL THEORY EXPLAINED

Reversal theory (Apter 1982, 1989) is an innovative approach in psychology to understanding human motivation and personality. As a phenomenologically based theory, it gives special emphasis to the complexity, changeability and inconsistency of the individual's behaviour and experience. Phenomenological approaches focus on the individual's unique perception and interpretation of events. Reversal theory thus provides an extensive but sound theoretical framework from which a credible explanation of soccer-related hooliganism can be developed. The purpose of this chapter is to review the fundamental concepts from reversal theory that are especially relevant to soccer hooliganism, a prerequisite to examining their application to the subject matter at hand.

The reversal theory approach

The structure of the person's subjective experience and the manner in which it may change over time is central to the theory's conceptual approach. In this respect, the person's subjective experience is closely related to both cognitive and emotional factors in human functioning. The phenomenological base of the theory has been called *structural phenomenology*, a label that reflects the theory's concern with experience and how it is structured.

The motive or motives underlying a person's behaviour may be different at different times. For example, a person setting out on a shopping expedition to replace an item of clothing may check on price and quality before finally making a purchase. The same individual, on another occasion, may go shopping with no particular purpose in mind and may purchase a similar item merely because the colour or style 'caught the eye', or the person 'fancied it at the time'. In this example, the behaviour (i.e. buying

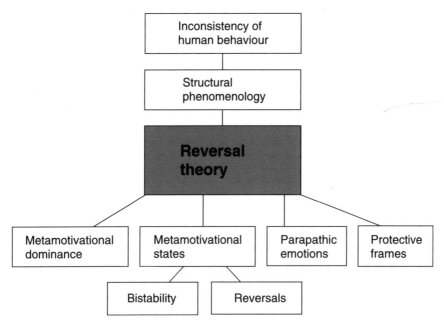

Figure 2.1 The main concepts in reversal theory relevant to the study of soccer hooliganism.

an item of clothing) is the same, but the underlying reasons for the behaviour are very different. In one case, buying the item of clothing (as a necessary replacement) was approached in a planned, serious goal-oriented manner, while in the second case the item was purchased in an spontaneous, impulsive manner.

In order to accommodate the changeable and inconsistent nature of human behaviour, a number of innovative concepts have been incorporated into the theory. These core concepts of *metamotivational states, reversals, bistability, state dominance, parapathic emotions* and *protective frames* are described in the following sections (see Figure 2.1).

Metamotivational states

As Murgatroyd (1985a) has pointed out, the term 'state' is used in psychology to describe something about a person at a particular moment in time, which is likely to be temporary and subject to change (e.g. 'angry', 'bored', 'serious'). The two different types of behaviour described in the example above are characteristic of one of the four pairs of opposite mental states that are thought, in reversal theory, to underpin motivation. Similarly, metamotivational states, as these psychological or mental states are known in reversal theory, are also liable to change.

Within the structural phenomenological approach, metamotivational states play a crucial role in the organization, structuring and interpretation of motives. The two metamotivational states associated with the shopping example are known as the *telic* and *paratelic* pair of states. For the person in the telic metamotivational state behaviour tends to be serious and planning-oriented (the carefully planned purchase). In the paratelic state, behaviour tends to be spontaneous, playful and present-oriented, with a preference for the pleasure of immediate sensation (the impulsive purchase). The shopping example illustrates basic differences in behaviour in the telic and paratelic metamotivational states.

Human behaviour, however, is often much more complex than that described in this straightforward example. Taking this example a stage further, most people will remember occasions when they went shopping for particular pre-planned items, perhaps even with the help of a shopping list, and once these items were acquired they returned home satisfied. In reversal theory terms, this shopping expedition comprised goal-oriented telic behaviour. Likewise, there may have been occasions when a person went out to buy a number of particular items but became distracted by, for example, a street theatre play, an exhibition or, perhaps, a cycling or marathon race taking place in the vicinity and failed to purchase the items. Here, a reversal from the telic state is likely to have taken place (see below) and the individual would then be enjoying these other events for their own sake, in the paratelic state. On any one shopping trip, or in any period in everyday life in general, reversals may occur quite frequently.

Four sets, or pairs, of metamotivational states (*telic–paratelic, negativism–conformity, sympathy–mastery, autic–alloic*) have been postulated by reversal theory. The characteristics of the telic–paratelic states have already been described and the others should, at this point, be clarified. When in the 'conformist' state, people generally feel the need to comply with, or conform to, an externally imposed requirement, as they might do when complying with a dress code in order to enter a restaurant or a night club. A person in the *negativistic* state feels the need to resist or rebel against an externally imposed requirement, by, for example, throwing litter on the street or walking on the grass in contravention of a sign which specifically asks people not to do so.

When in the mastery state, a person feels the need to master another person, group of people or object, like an instrument or machine. A musician learning to play an musical instrument is an example of someone who is probably in the 'mastery' state. Conversely, when in the sympathy state, sensitivity and tenderness and a feeling of giving are central to the experience. Nurses caring for the needs of patients in hospital may spend a good deal of their time in the 'sympathy' state. The autic–alloic pair of states focuses on a person's interaction with other people. In the autic state, people are concerned with what happens to themselves. In the alloic state, a person is more concerned with what happens to the other people with which he or she identifies. For example, a soccer player who has a specific role as a goal scorer and is in the autic state during a match might only be concerned with his or her own part and how it is received by the audience. By comparison, a team supporter in the crowd, in the alloic state, might feel satisfied when the team receive tumultuous appreciation from the crowd at the end of the match.

With these four metamotivational states (mastery–sympathy, autic–alloic), it is not *felt arousal* that is the important variable but a variable that Apter (1982) has termed *felt transactional outcome*. This is the degree to which a person perceives the outcome of a particular interaction in terms of net gain or loss. In the same way that there was an important relationship between felt arousal and hedonic tone for the *somatic metamotivational states*, there is a special relationship between felt transactional outcome and hedonic tone for the *transactional states*.

It is also hypothesized that combinations of metamotivational states from different pairs are operative at the same time. State combinations will be explored in more detail later, but it needs to be pointed out here that the 'salience' of the different metamotivational pairs will differ for different people. In other words, the centre of awareness for one person may be the autic–alloic pair while for another person the negativistic–conformity pair may be central.

Bistability

A bistable system is one that is said to operate between just two alternative preferred stable states at any one time. A simple example of a bistable system is provided by the temporary traffic lights that are often placed near road works and only have red or green lights. When one light is on, the other is off, and either one, red or green, represents a stable position. In reversal theory, the two opposite and mutually exclusive metamotivational states in any metamotivational pair are thought to exhibit bistability, thus allowing people to 'reverse' between opposite metamotivational states. The concepts of bistable and multistable systems, a related development in which there are many preferred stable states, have been taken from cybernetics.

Reversals

Reversals are the sudden changes or switches that occur between the operative metamotivational states in any one metamotivational pair. There are thought to be three different sets of conditions under which reversals can be triggered (see Figure 2.2). *Contingent events*, changes in some aspect of the person or the person's environment, can cause a reversal. For example, a motorcycle racer riding quickly around a motor circuit, in the paratelic state, suddenly hits a patch of oil on the surface of the racetrack

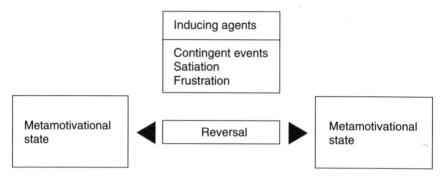

Figure 2.2 The reversal process with inducing agents.

and loses control, prompting a reversal to the telic state. Reversals may also take place as a result of a build up of frustration, when a person's needs are not being met in one particular metamotivational state. The golf player in the telic state, determined to practise putting on the practice green, may become so frustrated with his lack of success that a reversal takes place to the paratelic state and the golfer gives up and returns to the clubhouse. Third, the longer the time a person spends in one metamotivational state, the more likely he or she is to reverse as a result of satiation. The person who spends all morning 'working out' in a weight training facility in the telic state may reverse to the paratelic state, perhaps deciding to have a drink and a long lunch in a favourite restaurant. Reversals are, however, thought to be involuntary.

Incidentally, it should be emphasized that these examples are used merely to illustrate points or concepts from reversal theory. Judgements about people's behaviour based only on observation are liable to be erroneous. According to reversal theory, the person's subjective experience is crucial to any understanding of that person's behaviour at any particular time. As Svebak and Murgatroyd (1985: 107) pointed out,

> A main tenet of reversal theory is that a person can perform grossly similar behaviors on different occasions but have different metamotives for doing so. A person may drive a car at a very fast speed on one occasion in order to arrive on time at an important meeting; on another occasion their fast driving reflects their search for arousal and pleasure. The grossly similar behaviors performed on two occasions involve different metamotivational states.

Laboratory investigations have provided experimental support for reversal theory postulations about how these three types of inducing agents can bring about reversals. For example, Svebak *et al.* (1982) undertook an experiment which involved subjects completing a continuous perceptual motor task using a video game in which a car, manipulated by a joystick, had to be kept on a road viewed on a television screen. The results of experimental procedures, comprising threat and no-threat conditions, demonstrated that reversals to the telic state could be brought about through contingent events. Barr *et al.* (1990) induced and measured state reversals due to frustration in an experiment in which adult subjects tried to complete a puzzle. As there were more than 300,000 ways of combining the puzzle pieces incorrectly, and only one correct way of doing so, it was perhaps not surprising that the majority of the subjects became frustrated with the puzzle and reversed. Finally, Lafreniere *et al.* (1988) showed, using two types of computer tasks, statistics program and video games, that under unchanging laboratory conditions reversals due to satiation took place. Although three of the subjects did not reverse over the two-hour time period of the experiment, for the other twenty-six subjects spontaneous reversals occurred that could be attributed to satiation. That the reversals were prompted by satiation was confirmed by the comments of the subjects in detailed interviews held after the experiment.

State dominance

Metamotivational state dominance is a tendency to spend more time in one of the metamotivational states in any pair than the other. Some individuals thought to exhibit a bias towards, for instance, the negativistic state. They are labelled in the theory as *negativistic dominant*; conversely, those who show a bias towards the conformist state *conformist dominant*. The notion of dominance applies to all four pairs of metamotivational states. The idea of dominance in reversal theory should not be equated with the common notion in psychology of personality traits (e.g. Eysenck and Eysenck 1975). The trait approach to personality, which suggests that individuals behave in a consistent fashion, is at odds with the basic principle of reversal theory that human behaviour is inherently inconsistent. Dominance is a bias, not a permanent personality disposition consistent across all situations. Telic dominant individuals, for example, will still be subject to reversals and experience the paratelic state (see Murgatroyd 1985b). As McDermott (1988a: 297) stated,

> The theory does not equate 'dominance' with 'preference', however, since the state in which an individual is most frequently found to be is not necessarily the one in which he or she experiences the most pleasure. The concept of dominance is said to differ from that of 'trait' since the former does not assume that behaviour is consistent across situations. Rather the notion of dominance acknowledges that an individual may spend periods of time in the state of mind which is opposite to that which is 'dominant'.

Psychometric inventories have been developed that allow an individual's dominance with respect to, for example, the telic–paratelic and the negativism–conformity metamotivational pairs to be measured. These are the Telic Dominance Scale (Murgatroyd *et al.* 1978), which is comprised of three subscales (serious-mindedness, planning orientation and arousal avoidance) and the Negativism Dominance Scale (McDermott and Apter 1988), comprised of proactive and reactive negativism subscales. The development of measurement procedures that involve inventory techniques has, perhaps, made the differences between 'trait' and 'dominance' less clear. However, the use of other procedures, such as structured interviews (e.g. Svebak and Murgatroyd 1985) or psychophysiological techniques (e.g. Svebak 1985, for a review), has underlined the validity of dominance as a core concept in reversal theory.

Experiencing felt arousal

Felt arousal in reversal theory is 'the degree to which a person feels him or herself to be worked up at a given time'. In reversal theory, felt arousal is thought to be a crucial element in the motivation behind many human acts. The different ways in which people experience felt arousal can be illustrated by an examination of the relationship between felt arousal and the emotional feelings experienced in the telic and paratelic states. A person in the paratelic state usually prefers high levels of felt arousal, while someone in the telic state usually prefers low levels of felt arousal. In both cases, the experience is pleasant. Conversely, high levels of arousal in the telic and low levels of arousal in the paratelic state are likely to lead to unpleasant feelings (known as negative hedonic tone). Given that people may reverse between telic and paratelic states, the interaction of different levels of felt arousal and subsequent pleasant or unpleasant feelings leads to four emotional states. These are anxiety, excitement, boredom and relaxation as shown in Figure 2.3. If the telic state is operative, low felt arousal is experienced as pleasant relaxation. If, however, a reversal to the paratelic state takes place, then the person will experience low felt arousal as unpleasant boredom. High felt arousal in the paratelic state is usually experienced as pleasant excitement but, again, if a reversal takes place to the telic state, high felt arousal is then likely to be experienced by the person as unpleasant anxiety.

Reversal theory's interpretation of the experience of felt arousal challenges the theoretical stance of some other theories of motivation. The concept of bistability is at odds with, for example, the notion of homeostasis, which proposes that organisms are self-regulatory with only one preferred state. Optimal arousal theory (Hebb 1955: Berlyne 1967) is one psychological theory that incorporates the homeostatic concept. In this approach, individuals are thought to prefer arousal levels to be maintained at intermediate levels and strive to keep the homeostatic system balanced. Reversal theory, through the concept of bistability, argues that there are two equally stable preferred states between which the individual alternates. The

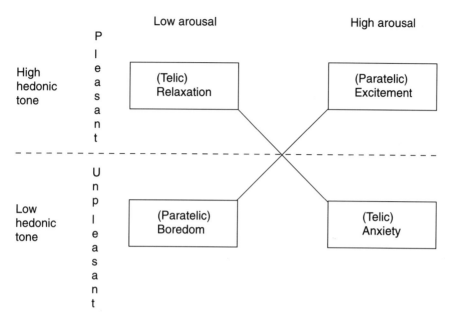

Figure 2.3 The different ways of experiencing felt arousal in the telic and paratelic states.

optimal arousal theory approach, although still prevalent in psychology, has distinct limitations, and has been subject to a good deal of criticism by reversal theorists and others (see Murgatroyd 1985a: 3; Kerr 1987; Apter 1989: 10).

Discrepancies between felt and preferred levels of a variable such as arousal and the way a person interprets them may lead to the development of unpleasant or stressful feelings (Apter and Svebak 1989).

Arousal seeking

Some people deliberately pursue high levels of felt arousal, which, under certain conditions, they can experience in a pleasant form as excitement.

In a number of situations, there may be a build-up of arousal in the telic state due to some threat, followed by a switch to the paratelic state when the threat is suddenly removed or overcome, the result being that the residual arousal is felt, before it decays, as excitement. Indeed this may be deliberately used as a way of obtaining pleasant high arousal. Hence, in many sports or other activities there may be a real danger, the overcoming of which produces feelings of high excitement before the arousal subsides: mountaineering, parachuting, and pot-holing would all be examples where there is real danger.'

(Apter 1982: 98)

The present author (Kerr 1985b, 1988a) has examined arousal seeking in anecdotal reports from participants in dangerous or risk sports which support the reversal theory view. In addition, a number of empirical studies have shown that 'risk' sport participants score higher on the arousal-seeking scale of the Telic Dominance Scale than non-participants or participants in 'safe' sports (see Kerr and Svebak 1989; Kerr, 1991). Other researchers have found similar results in other arousal-seeking activities: for example, real and laboratory gambling (Anderson and Brown 1984); variety of sexual behaviour (cited in Murgatroyd 1985b); choice of occupation, e.g. undercover drug agent (Girodo 1985); opiate addicts (Doherty and Matthews 1987). Kerr (1988b) has addressed the issue of arousal-seeking in soccer hooligans, a matter that is taken up again in Chapter 4. All of this is in keeping with reversal theory's stance that human behaviour is inconsistent and often paradoxical. This type of behaviour is paradoxical in the sense that, risking injury or death would seem to be completely at odds with biological survival.

Experiencing emotions: metamotivational state combinations

It is hypothesized within reversal theory that a person can experience combinations of different metamotivational states at any one particular time. Perhaps the easiest way of examining the various state combinations is to look, first, at the interaction of the telic–paratelic and negativistic-conformist pairs and then, second, at the interaction of the autic–alloic and sympathy–mastery pairs.

Simple calculations indicate that there are four possible state combinations: telic-negativism, paratelic-negativism, telic-conformity and paratelic-conformity. Earlier, the relationship between the telic and paratelic states was described as being rather like a set of traffic lights with only two lights, either one of which could be on at any time. It might be useful to think of the relationship between these four metamotivational states as being similar to a bank of two pairs of coloured theatre spotlights, used to illuminate a performance going on down below on stage. Again, although there are four different colours, let's say red and green, blue and yellow, only red or green and blue or yellow could be on at any one time. Therefore, the four coloured lights could be switched on in combination as red and blue, red and yellow, green and blue, green and yellow. These coloured lights represent the four possible two-way metamotivational combinations (see Figure 2.4).

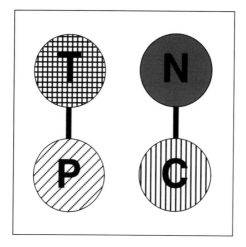

Figure 2.4 'Theatre lights' representing the telic–paratelic and negativism–conformity pairs of states and their possible combinations.

For example, a person taking a driving test, a serious activity, will be likely to conform to all traffic and driving rules or laws during the test and thus likely to have a *telic-conformist* combination of states operative. In fact if a 'learner' does not conform to traffic rules during the driving test, he or she will fail the test. Examples of *paratelic-conformist* behaviour can be found among people participating in game activities, where participants must 'play within the rules' but can enjoy the activity because of the novel and spontaneous nature of the play. Here the rules and the objectives of the game (e.g. to acquire money and property in the board game *Monopoly*) only serve to heighten paratelic excitement and enjoyment. Anti-nuclear protestors, such as the CND (Campaign for Nuclear Disarmament) in Britain in the 1960s and 1970s, or the anti-Vietnam War protestors in the United States, are likely examples of *telic-negativistic* behaviour. Here the individuals concerned thought that they were dealing with a serious problem and demonstrated actively against their governments and initial public pressure in order to achieve their goal. *Paratelic-negativism*, in contrast, is rebellious activity 'just for the hell of it', including activities such as causing trouble in class, refusing to wear school uniform or smoking on school premises, disobeying traffic laws, parking in forbidden zones or speeding, deliberately starting rows in pubs and arguing about politics with friends or colleagues for enjoyment. Arising from these different combinations and depending on felt arousal levels are eight primary emotions (called 'somatic' emotions in reversal theory): relaxation, anxiety, placidity, anger, excitement, boredom, provocativeness and sullenness (see Figure 2.5).

As mentioned earlier in this chapter, the mastery state is concerned with

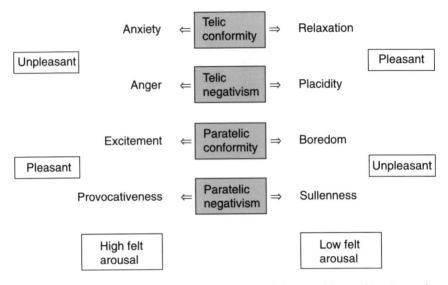

Figure 2.5 The eight somatic emotions generated by possible combinations of the telic–paratelic and negativism–conformity pairs of states.

trying to master a person or a situation, whereas the sympathy state involves perception on the part of the person concerned that something is being given. The autic and alloic states concern interaction or non-interaction with others. As with the telic–paratelic and negativistic–conformity pairs of metamotivational states, there are four possible state combinations that can arise from interactions of the second two metamotivational pairs: autic-mastery, alloic-mastery, alloic-sympathy and autic-sympathy. Returning to the analogy of the theatre lights, this second set of state combinations can be joined together with the first and might be thought of as a bank of four pairs of two different coloured lights of the type that can often be found in discos. Again, only one light from each pair (e.g. red–green, blue–yellow, purple–orange and pink–violet) can light up together with the one light from each of the other three pairs. Thus four lights can be on at any one time, representing a four-way state combination. One example might be telic-conformist-autic-mastery, another paratelic-negativistic-alloic-sympathy. One advantage of this analogy is that disco lights often seem to come on and off, for different lengths of time, in a manner similar to the way in which metamotivational state combinations are thought to work (see Figure 2.6).

Examples of the *autic-mastery* state combination are likely to be found in situations such as those where individuals take part as graduands in a university graduation day, receive a medal in the army, fly skilled and difficult movements with a remote-controlled model aircraft or successfully

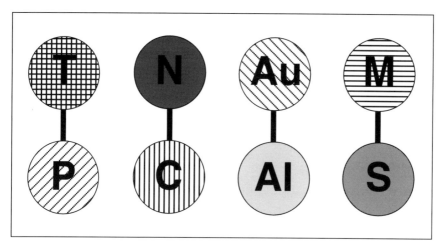

Figure 2.6 'Disco lights' representing all four pairs of metamotivational states and their possible combinations.

play a difficult bunker shot in golf. Being a member of a team trying to master another team in competition and being a spectator supporting a team are forms of behaviour likely to be undertaken with the *alloic-mastery* combination of states operative. *Autic-sympathy* makes up the likely combination of states during such activities as being allowed by your bank manager to run up an overdraft when you are financially hard up, being given a present or being told by someone that he or she likes you or receiving physiotherapy after injuring your back while playing badminton. Finally, the *alloic-sympathy* combination is likely to occur when the individual involves himself or herself in giving help to a close friend experiencing difficulty, sends a sympathy message to a family after a bereavement or sits down and helps a child with what is, for him or her, a difficult piece of homework.

Arising from these different combinations are another eight primary emotions (called 'transactional' emotions in reversal theory) emotions: pride, humiliation, gratitude, resentment, modesty, shame, virtue and guilt (see Figure 2.7).

There are a number of points in this discussion that need further elaboration. Depending on the levels of felt arousal and felt transactional outcome being experienced at any specific time, the strength and intensity of these different emotions will vary accordingly. In the disco lights analogy described earlier, the notion of strength and intensity of emotions is rather similar to the brightness and focus of the individual lights. As Apter (1985: 172) states,

> The relation between 'strength' and 'intensity' as the terms are used here in relation to emotion is not unlike the relation between the

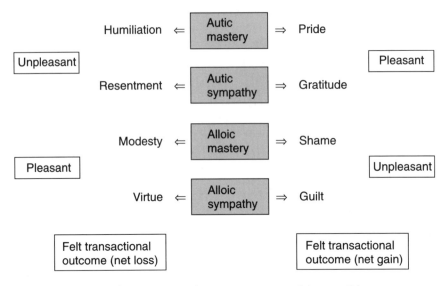

Figure 2.7 The eight transactional emotions generated by possible combinations of the autic–alloic and mastery–sympathy pairs of states.

saturation and the brightness of a colour. That is to say, the strength of an emotion is like the purity (i.e. saturation) of a colour while the intensity of an emotion is like the energy of the light source which emits the colour (i.e. its brightness). Hence, for example, it would be possible to feel pride in different degrees of strength – the emotion becoming clearer and purer as its strength increased – and also in different degrees of intensity; i.e. the emotion becoming associated with the more arousal as its intensity increased. Thus one could, for example, feel very proud while experiencing this in a relatively calm way, and also only a little proud while experiencing this in a way which could be described as 'worked up'.

Furthermore, these metamotivational combinations allow one state to enhance the experience of another. Consider, for example, the rock climber who repeatedly takes on more demanding climbs, thus placing himself or herself in more and more dangerous, anxiety-provoking situations. The climber may, if these increasingly difficult climbs are successfully negotiated, experience feelings of pride. In this example, the telic state enhances the feelings associated with the mastery state. Both types of state combination, somatic and transactional, influence the individual's experience at any one time. Thus, based on a combination of four different pairs of metamotivational states, from an overall constellation of sixteen possible emotions, one somatic and one transactional emotion (e.g. sullenness and resentment) will be experienced in conjunction.

Think also of the well-known Mexican Wave (which began during the 1986 World Cup held in Mexico) in which groups of seated spectators stand up, briefly swinging their arms above their heads and shouting before sitting down again, while the group next to them repeats the process. From a distance the impression of a roaring wave going right around the stadium is created. These waves are usually the spontaneous acts of the spectators. Those who participate in a Mexican Wave are likely to have the paratelic, conformist, alloic and mastery states operative: paratelic because it is spontaneous fun, conformist because people have to time their movements correctly if it is to work properly, mastery because they are involved in mastering the timing and movement of a task and alloic because they are part of something larger than themselves and it is for the sake of this that they are behaving in the way they are. Levels of felt arousal and felt transactional outcome will be relatively high and combine together to make the person feel pleased about what took place; a feeling that reversal theorists have called high 'self tone'.

Parapathic emotions and protective frames

The term parapathic emotion is used when a person perceives the emotion associated with a particular event within a *paratelic protective* frame. This allows unpleasant emotions, such as anger or fear, which are accompanied by high levels of felt arousal and experienced as unpleasant in the telic state, to be experienced as pleasant in the paratelic state. When watching a horror film, such as *Jaws*, *Dracula* or *Halloween*, people often experience the anxiety and fear associated with the often gruesome scenes, as a form of pleasant excitement. In different circumstances, feelings of guilt may add to the pleasures of activities like flirting, smoking in areas where it is forbidden, overeating, excessive drinking and driving at speed. Unpleasant emotions can, through this phenomenological reframing process, and provided a reversal to the telic state does not take place, be experienced in a pleasant, safe way. As Murgatroyd and Apter (1986: 265) have pointed out,

> What appears to happen to such 'negative' emotions as guilt, anger, fear, hate or horror is that a paratelic 'frame' is put around them so that they can be experienced playfully and the high arousal they generate is thus felt as pleasant. When such reframing occurs the resulting emotions are referred to within the theory as *parapathic emotions*.

People often seem deliberately to seek the pleasant experience of high arousal within a paratelic protective frame and have developed a number of different strategies for doing so while still feeling safe and secure (see

Apter 1982: 117–28). Those people who, for example, take part in dangerous sports are seeking the 'fear', excitement and high arousal experiences associated with such activities as mountaineering, ocean racing and motor racing (Kerr 1985a; Kerr and Svebak 1989). This type of activity can only be enjoyed if the 'real' (telic) fear normally associated with danger has been reinterpreted to an exhilarating experience by means of paratelic reframing. Remember that the paratelic experience is concerned with immediate gratification, a preference for spontaneity, a willingness to experiment, a preference for high arousal and a desire to prolong these type of activities. Although it is not of central concern to the present discussion, there are thought to be three separate types of protective frame, each of which is explained in detail in Apter (1992).

Closing comments

The phenomenological underpinnings of reversal theory mean that a main tenet of the theory is that people differ over time. People vary in the salience that different pairs of states and state combinations have for them. Some people will be more inclined to have certain states and combinations operative more often than other states. Within the constellation of emotions that reversal theory proposes, it is the manner in which emotions come together in their various combinations and the experience of these interactions that make people different. It is, however, certain combinations of metamotivational states and the resultant emotions that play a crucial role in the motivation of soccer hooligans. It is the task of this book to unravel these motivational processes as soccer hooligan behaviour is examined in detail in the following chapters.

References

Anderson, G. and Brown, R. I. F. (1984). 'Sensation-seeking and arousal in real and laboratory gambling'. *British Journal of Psychology*, 85, 401–10.

Apter, M. J. (1982). *The Experience of Motivation: the Theory of Psychological Reversals*. London: Academic Press.

Apter, M. J. (1985). 'Experiencing personal relationships', in M. J. Apter, D. Fontana and S. Murgatroyd (eds) *Reversal Theory: Applications and Developments*. Cardiff: University College Cardiff Press.

Apter, M. J. (1989). *Reversal Theory: Motivation, Emotion and Personality*. London: Routledge.

Apter, M. J. (1992). *The Dangerous Edge*. New York: The Free Press.

Apter, M. J. and Svebak, S. (1989). 'Stress from the reversal theory perspective', in C. D. Spielberger and J. Strelau (eds) *Stress and Anxiety, Vol. 12*. New York: Hemisphere, pp. 39–52.

Barr, S. A., McDermott, M. R. and Evans, P. (1990). 'Predicting persistence: a study of telic and paratelic frustration', in J. H. Kerr, S. Murgatroyd and M. J.

Apter (eds) *Advances in Reversal Theory*. Amsterdam: Swets and Zeitlinger, pp. 123–36.

Berlyne, D. (1967). 'Arousal and reinforcement', in D. Levine (ed.) *Nebraska Symposium on Motivation*. Lincoln, NE: University of Nebraska Press.

Doherty, O. and Matthews, G. (1987). 'Personality characteristics of opiate addicts'. *Personality and Individual Differences*, 9(1), 171–2.

Eysenck, H. J., and Eysenck S. B. G. (1975). *Manual of the Eysenck Personality Questionnaire*. London: Hodder and Stoughton.

Girodo, M. (1985). '*Telic and paratelic modes in operational undercover and field narcotics agents*'. Paper presented at the Second International Symposium on Reversal Theory, York University. Toronto, Canada, 23–26 May.

Hebb, D. O. (1955). 'Drives and the CNS (conceptual nervous system)'. *Psychological Review*, 62, 243–54.

Kerr, J. H. (1985a). 'The experience of arousal: a new basis for studying arousal effects in sports'. *Journal of Sports Sciences*, 3, 169–79.

Kerr, J. H. (1985b). 'A new perspective for sports psychology', in M. J. Apter, D. Fontana and S. Murgatroyd (eds) *Reversal Theory: Applications and Developments*. Cardiff: University College Cardiff Press, pp. 89–102.

Kerr, J. H. (1987). 'Structural phenomenology, arousal and performance'. *Journal of Human Movement Studies*, 13(5), 211–29.

Kerr, J. H. (1988a). 'Speed sports: the search for high arousal experiences'. *Sportswissenschaft*, 18(2), 185–90.

Kerr, J. H. (1988b). 'High arousal in football hooliganism', in M. J. Apter, J. H. Kerr and M. P. Cowles (eds) *Progress in Reversal Theory*. Amsterdam: North-Holland/Elsevier, pp. 223–30.

Kerr, J. H. (1991). 'Arousal-seeking in risk sport participants'. *Personality and Individual Differences*, 12(6), 613–16.

Kerr, J. H. and Svebak, S. (1989). 'Motivational aspects of preference for and participation in "risk" and "safe" sports'. *Personality and Individual Differences*, 10(7), 797–800.

Lafreniere, K., Cowles, M. P. and Apter, M. J. (1988). 'The reversal phenomenon: reflections on a laboratory study', in M. J. Apter, J. H. Kerr and M. P. Cowles (eds) *Progress in Reversal Theory*. Amsterdam: North-Holland/Elsevier, pp. 257–66.

McDermott, M. R. (1988a). 'Measuring rebelliousness: the development of the negativism dominance scale', in M. J. Apter, J. H. Kerr and M. P. Cowles (eds) *Progress in Reversal Theory*. Amsterdam: North-Holland/Elsevier, pp. 297–312.

McDermott, M. R. and Apter, M. J. (1988). 'The negativism dominance scale', in M. J. Apter, J. H. Kerr and M. P. Cowles (eds) *Progress in Reversal Theory*. Amsterdam: North-Holland/Elsevier, pp. 373–6.

Murgatroyd, S. (1985a). 'Introduction to reversal theory', in M. J. Apter, D. Fontana and S. Murgatroyd (eds) *Reversal Theory: Applications and Developments*. Cardiff: University College Cardiff Press, pp. 1–19.

Murgatroyd, S. (1985b). 'The nature of telic dominance', in M. J. Apter, D. Fontana and S. Murgatroyd (eds) *Reversal Theory: Applications and Developments*. Cardiff: University College Cardiff Press, pp. 20–41.

Murgatroyd, S. and Apter, M. J. (1986). 'A structural phenomenological approach to eclectic psychotherapy', in J. Norcross (ed.) *Handbook of Eclectic Psychotherapy*. New York: Brunner/Mazel.

Murgatroyd, S., Rushton, C., Apter, M. J. and Ray, C. (1978). 'The development of the Telic Dominance Scale'. *Journal of Personality Assessment*, **42**, 519–28.

Svebak, S. (1985). Psychophysiology and the paradoxes of felt arousal. In M. J. Apter, D. Fontana and S. Murgatroyd (eds) *Reversal Theory: Applications and Developments*. Cardiff: University College Cardiff Press, pp. 42–58.

Svebak, S., Storfjell, O. and Dalen, K. (1982). 'The effect of a threatening context upon motivation and task-induced physiological changes'. *British Journal of Psychology*, **73**, 505–12.

Svebak, S. and Murgatroyd, S. (1985). 'Metamotivational dominance: a multimethod validation of reversal theory constructs'. *Journal of Personality and Social Psychology*, **48**, 107–16.

3

THE PARATELIC NATURE
OF HOOLIGANISM
AND DELINQUENCY

Everyone has experienced a state of boredom at some time and for many people it is a regular, unpleasant aspect of their daily lives. Think, for example, of the young person trapped in an unstimulating school classroom:

> Sitting in a class for forty minutes, and hearing the teacher shouting at yer, and hearing the chalk on the board, BAM! – fifteen over four, fifteen times four – you get bored with it and you got nothing to say about it. So you say to your next-door neighbour, 'Arsenal played well Saturday, they should 'ave won'. The teacher catches you and sends you out. It's boring just sitting there, just looking at figures on a board, just copying 'em down.
>
> (Robins 1984: 103)

Klapp (1986) has listed seventy-one different words that can be used to describe the experience of boredom. He is one of those who thinks that many acts of hooliganism, vandalism and delinquency stem from boredom. Consider one of his examples, the case of Swiss youth, who on the face of it had all the material things they needed:

> Switzerland, regarded by many as a model country, gives a sharp picture of boredom affecting youth who were thought to have 'everything'. In Zurich in October 1980 a riot over the closing of a youth center 'crept across Switzerland, feeding on the restlessness of a young generation anxious to break out of a suffocating society'. Banners and graffiti in Lausanne proclaimed: 'We don't want a world where the guarantee of not dying from hunger is paid for by the certainty of dying from boredom.' A young man explained, 'We have everything – stereo, television, food, a place to sleep, everything. Our parents say, "here's some money, now go away." We want something else.'
>
> (Klapp 1986: 22)

In reversal theory, boredom is experienced when a person is in the paratelic state under conditions of low felt arousal, the level which is non-preferred in that state. The resulting mismatch in experienced felt arousal and preferred felt arousal leads to a build-up of tension that can be stressful. These unpleasant feelings are often promoted by monotonous, boring and non-stimulating conditions such as those found in the examples above, and in some types of repetitive work (Terkel 1973; Cox 1985).

Countering boredom

For many people, modulating arousal is the easiest way to alleviate boredom, and there are a whole host of activities to assist people to do this. One only has to think of video arcades, television game shows and 'soap' pro-grammes, gambling activities such as betting, lotteries and bingo, snooker rooms, shopping malls, pop music cassettes and videos, watching sports events and going out on a Saturday night after a monotonous and exhausting week's work. These are all examples of activities or places that allow people to attempt to cope with boredom by increasing felt arousal.

It seems likely that those people who perpetrate delinquent or hooligan acts may also be doing so to escape boredom by achieving metamotivational states in which high arousal can be enjoyed through paratelic functioning. Take, for example, the young people who engage in what has become known in Britain as 'joyriding'. In London between July 1987 and June 1988, 7,076 people were arrested for stealing and driving away cars. Of these, nearly one third were between the ages of ten and sixteen (Thompson 1988). Darren, aged thirteen and from Sunderland, is typical: 'Darren's record runs to burglary, robbery and assault. But mainly he steals cars – big, powerful motors which he drives at high speed and uses to ram police vehicles to avoid arrest' (Furbisher 1993). To observers (police, parents and others) joyriding is an extremely dangerous activity. Pedestrians and other road users are often killed or injured as a result of joyriders losing control of the car they are driving. To the joyriders, joyriding is a form of excitement or arousal seeking that they engage in purely for 'kicks'. Thompson (1988: 35) describes an interview with Alan, aged twenty-four, who stole his first car when he was eleven, but was not caught until he was eighteen: '"The first car I stole was a Rover 3500 SE. I'd been watching my dad driving and thought I could handle it," he says. "It was an automatic, so I just stuck it in Drive and went off. It was fantastic. I was doing wheel-spins, driving up and down at 70 miles an hour, screeching the tyres and everything – it was like a film."'

For bored and disaffected youth, joyriding provides a chance to experience immediate sensation in the form of excitement. Stealing the car, driving quickly, doing stunts and, if they are lucky, a car chase with the police all contribute to enhance the high arousal experience. Strange as it may seem, joyriding has been particularly prevalent among youths in Belfast, Northern Ireland. Given the presence of the security forces, one's first impression is that the young people involved are insane. On reflection, however, it becomes obvious that, for them, avoiding or trying to smash through police and army roadblocks, with the attendant possibility of being shot at, adds an extra dimension to the excitement of joyriding. The challenge offered by joyriding is used by youth to offset the effects of boredom. As Apter (1989: 152) stated,

> The delinquent – to turn to another conventional diagnostic category – can be seen as a youngster who is caught in the paratelic mode and in this respect is mode-inhibited. As a result he tends to treat everything – even things which others would take seriously, like the risk of physical danger or of arrest – as a kind of game . . . such concern as he does show is for immediate excitement, sensations, and gratifications such as loud rock music, drug-taking, and acts of gratuitous aggression. And his lifestyle is generally one of spontaneity and a lack of planning or thought for the future.

Although paratelic functioning and high arousal are not always associated with taking physical risks, some people are fortunate enough to have occupations where they are exposed to risks and thus from time to time they are able to enjoy levels of high felt arousal associated with paratelic functioning. Although for people such as firemen, soldiers and ambulance drivers there are long periods of mundane and perhaps boring work, the high risk activity at other times helps to offset boredom. In some cases, this experience may be gained through paratelic reframing and parapathic emotions. These risky jobs often attract paratelic dominant people who have a tendency deliberately to expose themselves to risks.

People, especially those who spend long periods in the paratelic state, unable to offset the effects of boredom through their jobs may have to adopt other strategies. In measurements using the Telic Dominance Scale (Murgatroyd *et al.* 1978), individuals who do expose themselves to the kinds of risks mentioned above have been found to be more paratelic dominant (i.e. less telic dominant) than individuals not involved in these types of activities. For example, police undercover narcotics agents (Girodo 1985), opiate drug users (Doherty and Matthews 1988) and risk sports participants (Kerr 1991) have all been found to show greater paratelic dominance. This was especially true for their scores on the arousal avoidance subscale, which were significantly lower than for subjects not involved in these activities. There is also empirical evidence which suggests that delinquents and soccer hooligans have a bias or tendency towards being impulsive, arousal seeking and generally paratelic dominant.

Research evidence: delinquents

Two samples of adolescent boys (n = 30), one group with a record of criminal behaviour, the other a control group with no history of delinquency, were incorporated in a study undertaken by McDonnell (1983). Subjects' scores on the Telic Dominance Scale (TDS) were compared. The delinquent group's scores on telic dominance were significantly lower (i.e. higher on paratelic dominance) than those of the control group, thus underlining arguments by Jones (1981) about the paratelic nature of much of what is categorized as delinquent behaviour.

Taking this line of research a stage further, Bowers (1985) administered the TDS to fifty-four adolescent boys, aged between 14 and 16.6 years and divided into three groups. The subjects in the first group (n = 20) all had a history of delinquency, including such offences as theft, burglary, handling stolen goods, taking and driving away cars, physical assault and possession of drugs. The second group (n = 14) were disruptive comprehensive school pupils who presented behaviour problems in the classroom but who had not committed offences that warranted police involvement. The third, control, group (n = 20) had no record of delinquency and did not present behaviour problems in school. The results indicated significant differences between groups on the planning orientation, arousal avoidance and overall telic dominance scores. In each case, the delinquent group's mean scores indicated greater paratelic dominance than the disruptive group's mean scores, which were in turn more paratelic than the control group's scores. Delinquent subjects showed less tendency to plan ahead (i.e. were more impulsive) than disruptive subjects and exhibited a greater tendency to operate on the spur of the moment. Disruptive subjects, although less impulsive than the delinquent group, were more impulsive than 'normal' school pupils (control group). A similar trend was observed with arousal-avoidance. The delinquent group scored lower on arousal-avoidance than the disruptive group. The disruptive group, in turn, scored higher than the 'normal' group, which showed the greatest tendency towards arousal avoidance. Thus, in addition to the results with the delinquent group, which confirm McDonnell's (1983) earlier findings, low telic dominance or a high tendency towards paratelic behaviour was also observed, although to a lesser extent, in disruptive school students who had no history of contravening the law.

A number of other research studies have linked impulsiveness, a characteristic of paratelic dominance, with delinquency. Eysenck and McGurk (1980), for example, used a number of trait personality questionnaires to study a population of 641 male delinquent subjects aged between 17 and 21 years (mean age 18.05 years) held at the Medomsly Detention Centre in County Durham in England. Statistical treatment of the results using factor analysis indicated the importance of 'impulsiveness' and 'venturesomeness' in delinquent behaviour. A link was found to exist between impulsiveness and psychotism and between venturesomeness and a component of 'extraversion' concerned with risk-taking. The authors argued that impulsiveness may be caused by a non-evaluation of the situation, typical of individuals who score high on psychotism, and venturesomeness may be caused by conscious decisions to take risks, a characteristic of extraverted behaviour.

In addition, they suggested that the most impulsive individuals will be the most 'at risk' in terms of anti-social behaviour.

Thornton (1985) considered delinquency to be a form of risk-taking, and carried out an empirical study in which he investigated the rate of offending, risk evaluations and risk-preferences of 276 male detention centre trainees (aged from 14 to 16 years) drawn from three centres in the south of England. He incorporated the venturesomeness and impulsiveness items (Eysenck and Eysenck 1978) also used by Eysenck and McGurk (1980) and a self-report delinquency scale. Overall, the results showed that high-rate offenders were characterized by both high-risk preference and a tendency not to evaluate risks before acting. Impulsiveness was found to be related to self-reported rate of offending, as well as differentiating between convicted delinquents and 'normal' subjects. As Thornton (1985: 128) pointed out, 'The gains from crime are fairly immediate whereas the costs associated with it for the offender are more remote, so it is reasonable to expect that people who act without stopping to think will be more likely to commit offences.'

Dahlbäck (1990) has argued that people have individual preferences for taking risks, and that these preferences might differ, depending on the importance of the decision. Using Swedish students as subjects, his study supported the hypothesis that criminality and risk-taking have a positive relationship with each other. In addition, this relationship was shown to be stronger for crimes where the chance of detection was less likely than for crimes where the probability of detection was greater.

Farley and Sewell (1976) undertook a study in which they tested the notion that the delinquent has an exaggerated need for stimulation. Using Zuckerman's Sensation Seeking Scale (Zuckerman *et al.* 1964), an instrument which has a close correlational relationship with the Telic Dominance Scale (see Murgatroyd 1985), they examined differences in Sensation Seeking Scale scores for black American male and female delinquents and non-delinquents. Their results indicated that sensation-seeking is positively correlated with juvenile delinquency. Haapasalo (1990) obtained similar results in a study of Finnish prison inmates and non-offenders when he used both Zuckerman's Sensation Seeking Scale and the Eysenck Personality Questionnaire (Eysenck and Eysenck 1975). He found that overall sensation seeking scores were higher for offenders than for non-offenders. Furthermore, offenders scored higher on the Eysenck neuroticism and lie scales and lower than non-offenders on the extraversion scale.

In a study carried out by Arnett (1990), drunk driving behaviour in 181 seventeen- and eighteen-year-old American males was found to be significantly related to sensation seeking. With Zuckerman's Sensation Seeking Scale, significant relationships were found in both the overall sensation seeking score and the thrill and adventure seeking, disinhibition and boredom susceptibility subscales. Arnett (1990) suggested that the motivation behind drunk driving was at least partly attributable to the person's propensity for sensation seeking. Disinhibition may be combined with the loosening of a young person's inhibitions, following sensation seeking alcohol use, which may then subsequently lead to drunk driving.

A national poll of US teenagers found that some 25 per cent reported that they had shoplifted (Gallup 1980), and while only 21 per cent of these subjects said they shoplifted 'for the money', 72 per cent said they did it for 'kicks'. Moreover, Donnermeyer and Phillips (1984) report the findings of an investigation that asked 572 fifteen- and sixteen-year-old teenagers in Ohio about their involvement in acts of vandalism. Based on the self-reports of these young people, Donnermeyer and Phillips (1984: 155–6) were led to conclude 'that a majority of those who had committed an act of vandalism became involved because they "just happened to be there", "were bored", "playing around", or "pressured by others" . . . In essence, involvement was unplanned and, in many cases, spontaneous'.

Research evidence: soccer hooligans

Arousal-seeking and risk-taking aspects of paratelic behaviour are so important in the context of soccer hooliganism that Chapter 4 is devoted to examining the processes involved in some detail. Research evidence from Germany and Belgium underlines the link between seeking arousal and taking risks and hooligan behaviour at soccer matches.

Gabler (1984) incorporated several different methods of collecting data into his study of the behaviour of VfB Stuttgart 'fans' during the 1979–80 soccer season in West Germany. In addition to information available from police telex dispatches sent when trouble occurred at matches, eighty-five policemen and 510 stewards completed questionnaires and a team of six participant observers collected material. These participant observers travelled to and from home and away games with fans and attended social activities organized by groups of fans during the week. The study identified the special nature of the emotional experience of soccer 'fans' attending these matches. Fans appeared to experience 'states of being' as part of an overall 'broad affective activation', during which they reported feelings of joy, pleasure, satisfaction and grief. While some fans appeared satisfied by the attraction of 'lots of things going on', for others (the hooligans) confrontation with stewards and police was found to be the main focus of their need for high sensation or arousal. Of the subjects interviewed, 20 per cent deliberately sought out dangerous situations, a by-product of which was often aggression. As Gabler (1984: 7) stated, 'In our understanding, the sensation-seeking motive was the most important motive for the fans to visit the match . . . It is the explicit aim of many fans to bring themselves into situations that contain adventures, action, tension, risk and dangers.'

Similar findings were reported by Van Limbergen *et al.* (1987), who carried out an empirical study on football hooliganism in first class soccer in Belgium during the 1986–7 soccer season. This research was carried out under instruction from the Belgian Council of Ministers by the Youth

Criminology Research Group at the University of Leuven in close co-operation with the state police and the Ministry of Internal Affairs. As in Gabler's (1984) study, a number of different empirical methods were used to obtain information. These included semi-structured interviews with thirty-three of the recognized hooligans from those clubs with strong hooligan elements (Anderlecht, Antwerp and Bruges) and participant observation at matches where hooligan trouble was considered likely. In addition, information was obtained from dossiers on individual hooligans held by the public prosecutors' office, the Belgian football authorities (KBVB), the soccer clubs and fan material (e.g albums of press cuttings). Among their conclusions, the researchers found that one of the major motivating factors for Belgian soccer hooligans was the excitement associated with the acts of violence and hooliganism and the risks involved in the 'war games' with other hooligans and the police.

The research findings outlined above suggest that across a number of different cultures, fundamental aspects of delinquency and hooliganism are associated with paratelic dominance. It seems that people who engage in these activities may be satisfying their need for stimulation through forms of antisocial behaviour that involve risk and novel or varied situations. In some cases, this antisocial behaviour may develop to a level that can be classified as a psychopathic disorder (Farrington 1991). With respect to soccer hooligans, this is only likely to be true in the case of the extreme types: the hardmen and superthugs. This topic is returned to and dealt with in more detail in Chapter 7.

Performing delinquent and hooligan acts

An important investigation, which underlines the complexity of the motivation behind acts of delinquency, vandalism and hooliganism, was carried out by Jones and Heskin (1988). This study attempted to provide a more detailed knowledge of the individual's interpretation of the meaning or purpose of his or her own behaviour.

Twenty-one young males (aged thirteen to sixteen years) attending an open school for juvenile offenders were the subjects of this comprehensive study. Five structured interviews were held with these subjects at six-weekly intervals for a period of eighteen months, and non-structured interviews were held with the remaining subjects (n = 16) over an eight-month period. In addition, psychological, psychiatric and social work reports and ongoing school staff reports were used to provide additional information. The authors concluded from the available data that delinquent acts were brought about by a multiplicity of consequences linked in a 'complex interplay of social, historical and situational variables' (p. 37). Basing the analysis of their results on reversal theory principles, Jones and Heskin (1988) identified a four-category framework, which is linked directly via feedback loops through metamotivational state to the person and the delinquent act. This four-category framework included both positive and negative reinforcing or punishing events depending on the interpretation of the particular subject. The various categories within the framework, along with other aspects of the authors' functional analysis, are shown in Figure 3.1.

The positive reinforcement category concerns the presentation of a stimulus or stimuli contingent on a response that serves to increase the frequency of that response. Examples of such acts from their research included being involved in a high speed car chase during joyriding and purse snatching in which part of the contents were removed and the purse was replaced in the owner's handbag. The positive reinforcing nature of the particular act (associated with the level of risk or difficulty) is evident from subjects' reported feelings of elation or being 'high', of increased peer group status or self-esteem.

Conversely, negative reinforcement is to do with the withdrawal of an aversive stimulus (or stimuli) in terms of, for example, release from peer group pressure (sometimes bullying) and group norms, which often manifests itself in the carrying out of delinquent acts with a lack of regard for possible arrest. One example described by the authors involved a subject who remained on the roof of a burgled house until the police arrived and then proceeded to bombard them with roof tiles. Jones and Heskin (1988) argued that in some cases, such as bullying as described above, imprisonment may function as a reinforcing stimulus for delinquent behaviour. Finally, the most interesting conclusion from the results in the third and fourth categories, positive and negative punishments (to do with presentation or withdrawal of a stimulus, contingent on a response that serves to decrease the frequency of that response), was that subjects' attitudes and behaviour remained largely unaffected by being placed in a special school or having further loss of privileges as a result of further delinquent behaviour while at the school.

This study and the arguments presented in the interpretation of the results are important. By beginning to unravel the complexity of the motivation behind acts of delinquency, hooliganism or vandalism, they direct attention to the search for a more sophisticated understanding of the problem. Although Jones and Heskin's (1988) work was a step forward, they did not specify which metamotivational states or combinations of states were involved in the types of behaviour grouped in their different categories. For instance, much of the behaviour in the positive reinforcement category would be recognized by reversal theorists as being associated with high levels of felt arousal and felt transactional outcome characteristic of a metamotivational combination of paratelic, negativistic, autic and mastery states. Much of the behaviour in the negative reinforcement category would also seem to be especially linked to the transactional emotions arising from a metamotivational combination of alloic-mastery. This may be a means of improving feelings of self-tone, necessary as a result of peer group pressure and previously low levels of felt transactional outcome. Paratelic-negativism would also seem to be combined with alloic-mastery in, for example, the

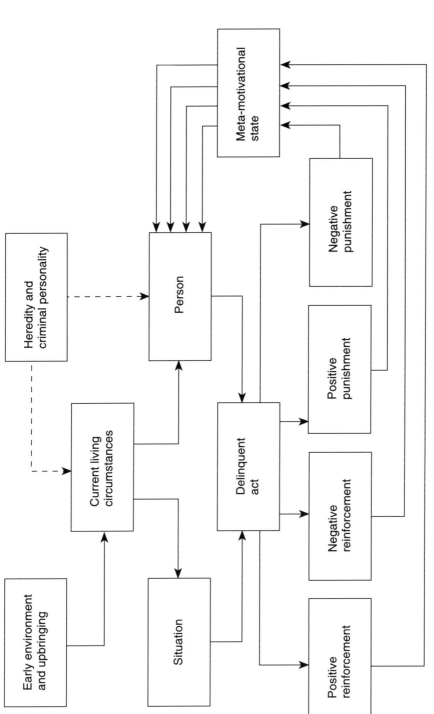

Figure 3.1 Functional analysis of delinquent behaviour. Dotted lines represent the unverifiable nature of hypothetical constructs related to hereditary and criminal personality. From Jones and Heskin (1988).

case of the boy who carried out the burglary and then played the game on the roof with the police.

By adopting reversal theory explanations of why these acts occur, especially the influence of different combinations of metamotivational states, we might gain a greater insight into the mental processes that produce, direct and sustain delinquent and hooligan behaviour. Similar arguments to those of Jones and Heskin (1988) have been made by Brown (1988) in his work on human addictions such as gambling and alcoholism (see Chapter 7).

The pleasure of being destructive

The role of arousal, experienced pleasure and reinforcement in this regard should not be underestimated. Examination of the specific nature of one act of vandalism and hooliganism in more detail, however, may reveal how this motivational experience is facilitated. Being destructive, for instance, as delinquents and soccer hooligans often are, can in itself be an enjoyable experience. Allen (1984) has linked the feelings of enjoyment associated with an act of destruction with the similar pleasant feelings that may be realized from an aesthetic experience. He argued that the enjoyment associated with socially accepted activities such as art, music and literature is generated by the same feelings of positive hedonic tone associated with more socially unacceptable acts of destruction. He went on to point out that if vandalism can be linked to theories of aesthetics (Berlyne 1971), then levels of arousal experienced as positive hedonic tone can be increased by a number of 'collective' stimulus properties. Thus, breaking an object will be experienced as more enjoyable by the individual if qualities of 'complexity', 'expectation', 'uncertainty' and 'novelty' can be introduced. In a series of research studies (e.g. Allen and Greenberger 1978, 1979), Allen obtained results consistent with his arguments and predictions. Significant positive correlations were found between the degree of enjoyment during destruction and the characteristics of the process of destruction, such as complexity, interestingness, expectedness and level of excitement. Other studies (e.g. Lewis and Allen 1982) examined auditory rather than visual aspects of breaking objects and found similar correlations between the degree of enjoyment and sounds produced during the destruction. Extending what he terms 'aesthetic or hedonic theory' to causality in vandalism, Allen (1984) argued that acts of vandalism are likely to be invoked by three types of cues: first, the appearance of particular objects in the environment; second, an individual's anticipation of the forthcoming hedonic experience during the destructive act; third, anticipation of the appearance of the object after destruction. He goes on to say that,

> Furthermore, even if vandalism were produced by motives that are totally extraneous to this theory (e.g. imitation or revenge) the hedonic experience would still reinforce destructive behavior and thus increase

the likelihood of vandalism occurring again. Since degree of enjoyment in destruction varies across different acts, intermittent reinforcement is produced; and as we know, such a pattern produces strong resistance to extinction.

(Allen 1984: 87)

Beyond situational versus trait explanations

In spite of the widespread appeal of personality theories of crime and juvenile delinquency to some observers and of the situational approach to others (Borrill 1983), it should be kept in mind that reversal theory is about the inconsistency of human behaviour.

For some observers, the view that hooligans and criminals have a personality disposition, which places the blame for their behaviour on a hidden aberration, is a somewhat comfortable view that to a large extent excuses society (Borrill 1983: 127). Alternatively, placing the blame on situational factors in the environment that influence people's decisions to commit hooligan and delinquent offences excuses the individual. As McDermott (1992) said, 'The danger of taking an exclusively personality-based approach is that it may let society "off the hook". The danger of not taking such an approach is that it may let the individual "off the hook"'.

Reversal theory bridges the gap between these two approaches and takes the debate about hooliganism and delinquency beyond the level of personality disposition versus situational factors. Within the theory's constructs, the notion of metamotivational dominance is merely an innate bias in people to operate in one of a pair of metamotivational states rather than the other and is not as restrictive and fixed as the notion of a personality disposition or trait. The behaviour of people classified as extraverts, for example, is expected to be consistently extraverted, whereas someone who is, for example, negativistic-dominant will also spend time in the conformist state. Reversal theory also goes beyond the idea that behaviour is situationally consistent. This means that the soccer hooligan who on one occasion smashes a shop window may on another occasion, in exactly the same situation, do something completely different. Thus, reversal theory provides a conceptual framework that, as it were, excuses neither the individual nor society and keeps both 'on the hook'.

Closing comments

Arguments in this chapter have tried to show that one of the key elements is likely to be a combination of the soccer hooligan's paratelic dominance and discrepancies between preferred and actual levels of felt arousal in the paratelic state (as a result of being frequently bored), which influence behaviour and lead to hooligan acts as a means of compensation.

Perhaps Elias and Dunning (1970) were close to the truth in their essay 'The quest for excitement in unexciting societies'. They argued that in the more advanced industrial societies, opportunities for individuals or communal groups to experience excitement have become less frequent. In addition, by comparison with earlier societies, the means, both sociological and psychological, of restraining public expressions are thought to be stronger. This is considered by the authors to be symptomatic of the civilizing process, as is the decreasing influence of religion as a 'balancing relaxation of restraints'. The type of excitement found in leisure activities, such as sport, music, drama, gambling or rock and roll, is considered to be a comparatively civilized type of excitement. Within this framework, the soccer match could be seen as providing the setting for people to escape from the social constraints and control of everyday life, to experience excitement and to express their emotions freely:

> In societies such as ours which require an all-round emotional discipline and circumspection, the scope for strong pleasurable feelings openly expressed is severely hedged in. For many people it is not only in their occupational but also in their private lives that one day is the same as the other. For many of them, nothing new, nothing stirring ever happens. Their tension, their tonus, their vitality, or whatever one might call it is thus lowered. In a simple or a complex form, on a low or a high level, leisure time activities provide, for a short while, the upsurge of strong pleasurable feelings which is often lacking in ordinary routines of life. Their function is not simply as is often believed, a liberation from tensions, but the restoration of that measure of tension which is an essential ingredient of mental health. The essential character of their cathartic effect is the restoration of a normal mental 'tonus' through a temporary and transient upsurge of pleasurable excitement.
>
> Elias and Dunning (1970: 50)

In the next chapter, the soccer environment will be examined in some detail to show how both soccer fans and hooligans have adopted a variety of strategies for facilitating pleasant high arousal experience.

References

Allen, V. L. (1984). 'Toward an understanding of the hedonic component of vandalism', in C. Levy-Leboyer (ed.) *Vandalism: Behaviour and Motivations.* Amsterdam: North-Holland, pp. 77–89.

Allen, V. L. and Greenberger, D. B. (1978). 'An aesthetic theory of vandalism'. *Crime and Delinquency,* **24**, 309–22.

Allen, V. L. and Greenberger, D. B. (1979). 'Enjoyment of destruction: the role of uncertainty'. *Journal of Non-verbal Behavior,* **4**, 87–96.

Apter, M. J. (1982). *The Experience of Motivation: the Theory of Psychological Reversals*. London and New York: Academic Press.

Apter, M. J. (1989). *Reversal Theory: Motivation, Emotion and Personality*. London: Routledge.

Arnett, J. (1990). 'Drunk driving, sensation seeking, and egocentrism among adolescents'. *Personality and Individual Differences*, 11(6), 541–6.

Berlyne, D. E. (1971). *Aesthetics and Psychobiology*. New York: Appleton-Century-Crofts.

Borrill, J. (1983). 'Psychology and crime', in J. Nicholson and B. Foss (eds), *Psychology Survey 4*. Leicester: British Psychological Society, pp. 109–36.

Bowers, A. J. (1985). 'Reversals, delinquency and disruption'. *British Journal of Clinical Psychology*, 25, 303–4.

Brown, R. I. F. (1988). 'Reversal theory and subjective experience in the explanation of addiction and relapse', in M. J. Apter, J. H. Kerr and M. P. Cowles (eds), *Progress in Reversal Theory*. Amsterdam: North-Holland/Elsevier, pp. 191–211.

Cox, T. (1985). 'Repetitive work: occupational stress and health', in C. L. Cooper and M. J. Smith (eds) *Job Stress and Blue Collar Work*. Chichester: John Wiley & Sons, pp. 85–112.

Dahlbäck, O. (1990). 'Criminality and risk-taking'. *Personality and Individual Differences*, 11(3), 265–72.

Doherty, O., and Matthews, G. (1988). 'Personality characteristics of opiate addicts'. *Personality and Individual Differences*, 9(1), 171–2.

Donnermeyer, J. F. and Phillips, G. H. (1984). 'Vandals and vandalism in the USA: a rural perspective', in C. Levy-Leboyer (ed.) *Vandalism: Behaviour and Motivations*. Amsterdam: North-Holland, pp. 149–60.

Elias, N. and Dunning, E. (1970). 'The quest for excitement in unexciting societies', in G. Luschen (ed.) *A Cross-cultural Analysis of Sports and Games*. Champaign, IL: Stipes, pp. 31–51.

Eysenck, H. J. and Eysenck, S. B. G. (1975). *Manual of the Eysenck Personality Questionnaire*. London: Hodder and Stoughton.

Eysenck, S. B. G. and Eysenck, H. J. (1978). 'Impulsiveness and venturesomeness: their positions in a dimensional system of personality description'. *Psychological Reports*, 43, 1247–55.

Eysenck, S. B. G. and McGurk, B. J. (1980). 'Impulsiveness and venturesomeness in a detention center population'. *Psychological Reports*, 47, 1299–306.

Farley, F. H. and Sewell, T. (1976). 'Test of an arousal theory of delinquence: stimulation-seeking in delinquent and non-delinquent black adolescents'. *Criminal Justice and Behavior*, 3, 314–20.

Farrington, D. P. (1991). 'Antisocial personality from childhood to adulthood'. *The Psychologist: Bulletin of the British Psychological Society*, 4, 389–94.

Furbisher, J. (1993). 'Darren, 13, rides green lights of the law into criminal legend'. *The Sunday Times*, 14 February, 5.

Gabler, H. (1984). 'On the problem of soccer spectators' aggressions'. Paper presented at the Olympic Scientific Congress, Eugene, OR, USA.

Gallup, G. (1980). 'Teen thievery is a major trend'. *Columbus Dispatch*, February. Cited in Donnermeyer and Phillips (1984).

Girodo, M. (1985). 'Telic and paratelic modes in operational undercover and field narcotics agents'. Paper presented at the second International Conference on Reversal Theory, York University, Toronto, Canada.

Haapasalo, J. (1990). 'Sensation seeking and Eysenck's personality dimensions in an offender sample'. *Personality and Individual Differences*, 11(1), 81–4.

Jones, R. (1981). 'Reversals, delinquency and fun'. *European Journal of Humanistic Psychology*, 9, 237–40.
Jones, R. S. P. and Heskin, K. J. (1988). 'Towards a functional analysis of delinquent behaviour: a pilot study'. *Counselling Psychology Quarterly*, 1(1), 35–42.
Kerr, J. H. (1991). 'Arousal seeking in risk sport participants'. *Personality and Individual Differences*, 12, 613–16.
Klapp, O. E. (1986). *Overload and Boredom*. New York: Greenwood Press.
Lewis, S. and Allen, V. L. (1982). *Sounds of Destruction*. Unpublished manuscript.
McDermott, M. R. (1992). Personal communication.
McDonnell, V. (1983). 'Telic dominance, interpersonal relations and delinquency'. Unpublished project report, Cambridge Institute of Education.
Murgatroyd, S. (1985). 'The nature of telic dominance', in M. J. Apter, D. Fontana and S. Murgatroyd (eds) *Reversal Theory: Applications and Developments*. New York: Lawrence Erlbaum, pp. 20–41.
Murgatroyd, S., Rushton, C., Apter, M. J. and Ray, C. (1978). 'The development of the Telic Dominance Scale'. *Journal of Personality Assessment*, 42, 519–28.
Robins, D. (1984). *We Hate Humans*. Harmondsworth: Penguin.
Terkel, S. (1973). *Working*. New York: Pantheon.
Thompson, T. (1988). 'Joyride? You mean deathride'. *The Observer*, 6 November, 35.
Thornton, D. (1985). 'Rate of offending, risk evaluation and risk preference'. *Personality and Individual Differences*, 6(1), 127–8.
Van Limbergen, K., Colaers, C. and Walgave, L. (1987). 'Onderzoek naar de maatschappelijke en psycho-sociale achtergronden van het Voetbalvandalisme'. (Research into the social and psychosocial background of football hooliganism'). Katholieke Universiteit Leuven, Belgium.
Zuckerman, M., Kolin, A., Price, L. and Zoob, I. (1964). 'Development of a sensation seeking scale'. *Journal of Clinical Psychology*, 28, 477–82.

4

SOCCER AND THE
PURSUIT OF EXCITEMENT

As mentioned in the Preface, the words 'fan' and 'supporter' are used interchangeably for people, often with an allegiance to a particular team, who watch soccer. The term 'soccer hooligan' is reserved for those attending soccer matches who engage in aggression and violence. Others have not made this distinction so clearly and sometimes the words 'fan' and 'supporter' are used in situations which clearly involve hooligan acts. This chapter examines the activities of both fans and hooligans in their pursuit of excitement at soccer games.

The soccer environment provides a rich source of varied experience for those who wish to pursue and enjoy the feelings of pleasant high arousal associated with excitement. People in general develop their own personal strategies for modulating felt arousal, including such everyday examples as eating, smoking tobacco and drinking coffee (see Thayer 1989). Moreover, people may be more astute than they realize at placing themselves in situations or environments which they know from experience will provide them with pleasant high felt arousal experiences. Apter (1991) grouped a number of psychological strategies for obtaining high felt arousal experiences into seven general categories. Achieving high arousal is possible through: (a) exposing oneself to arousing stimulation; (b) empathy with the characters depicted in fiction and narrative; (c) accepting any kind of challenge; (d) novel or unexpected events; (e) deliberate and provocative negativism; (f) the experience of arousing contrasting effects; (g) facing danger within a protective frame. These different strategies are examined here in the context of soccer. First, strategies used by regular soccer fans, within the usual features of the soccer environment (stategies a, b, d, f and g), will be discussed. Second, strategies associated specifically with the activities of soccer hooligans will be highlighted (all seven strategies above). They are separated in the discussion here for convenience. Hooligans, to some extent, also use the strategies of the regular fans, but these are insufficient to satisfy the needs of the hooligans, so they have developed their own more extreme variety.

Soccer fan strategies

By attending a soccer game, people voluntarily and deliberately place themselves in a situation abundant in arousing stimulation, in which high arousal is an intrinsic aspect of the event. Actually being in a crowd, especially one at a sports event, can be exciting in itself. The excitement that begins to build up on the way to the soccer game (Roadburg 1980: 269) is increased by the noise, colour and other forms of intense stimulation. During the game, if the teams are well matched or are engaged in an intriguing tactical battle, this adds greatly to the high arousal soccer experience. In Britain, for example, the style of play is generally recognized as being fundamentally different from that in other countries. This 'cut and thrust' or, as it is sometimes termed, 'end to end' style provides extra thrills and sensation, in what are often highly dramatic encounters.

At the game there are also specific forms of fan behaviour that are geared to increase the intensity of colour and noise as sources of stimulation. Morris (1981), in his book *The Soccer Tribe*, includes a section on the displays of the followers. Images of the flag waving, paper and streamer 'storms' and scarf displays of soccer fans are captured in a number of remarkable colour photographs. Remarkable though they are, these photographs cannot really convey the emotional intensity that results from seeing or being involved in such activities 'live' at a game, such as standing on the Kop at Liverpool (see Clarke 1973: 9). Spectators' scarf displays have been especially popular in England. Marsh (1978a) pointed out that scarves (in the appropriate team colours) worn by soccer fans are often tied around the wrist and not around the neck. As a result, when hands are raised in triumph, or for the purpose of rhythmic clapping (see below), a collective mass of colour, visible to all, but especially to rival supporters, is raised aloft.

Chanting and rhythmic clapping

Marsh's (1978a) research included an analysis of soccer chants, with details of chanting at a number of English first division soccer games in the 1978–9 season. He suggested that many of the chants (on average 147 per game) were unrelated to incidents in the game and were often initiated when the play was boring and the crowd had lost some of its mood of excitement. Further research on crowd chants at fifteen Oxford United home matches revealed that chants, usually initiated by a chant leader, could be classified in a number of different categories (Marsh 1982). These included chants concerned with winning, confidence and optimism, team or player encouragement or praise, team loyalty and pride, team or player criticism (usually but not exclusively directed at the opposition team), insults directed at the referee, police or opposition (the most popular form of chanting), threats directed at the opposition, in celebration of game disruption or pseudo-rivalry (between different sections of similar fans during boring or dull matches). A final category lacked any specific message and appeared to be solely for helping to create an exciting atmosphere. Marsh went on to point out that chants were short and simple, and allowed endless repetition and increasing numbers of fans to join in, thus increasing the rhythm until the noise level reached a crescendo.

Soccer supporters' loud and rhythmic chanting in unison is, of course, highly arousing. In addition, the variety of chants, along with new inventions and the adaptation of older versions, provide a degree of novelty that also contributes to the overall arousing effect. The chanting and singing by rival fans at games provides an example of one group challenging the other. The challenge here is on two levels: first, in terms of the quality, variety and originality of the chants; second, in terms of the threats that often form the contents. Chanting is not confined to soccer stadia but is also often used during travel to games to shock ordinary bystanders, or in an attempt to frighten or challenge rival fans:

> Station concourses are terrific places for chanting. There might be seven hundred people emerging from a train full of booze, hope and expectation. 'Arsenal, Arsenal' would echo through the high-roofed buildings, a crescendo of noise reverberating around the station. It used to deafen us and frighten the hell out of any poor soul who happened to be catching a train. We marched out of the station like young gladiators.
>
> (Ward 1989: 10)

Marsh (1978a) reported investigations using slow-motion camera analysis, which have been carried out on the rhythmic or synchronous clapping that often accompanies or is integrated with rhythmic chanting at soccer games. Synchronous clapping on the soccer terraces has three main features. It is usually performed with the hands held high over the head and follows a clear rhythmic pattern, highly synchronized between fans. Following analysis of the slow-motion film, practically all the fans on view were found to have their hands in identical positions at a specific time: the 'degree of error' was only a few inches and level of the synchronization was remarkable. Although these forms of rhythmic chanting and clapping would appear have originated in and remain largely confined to Britain, South American soccer crowds, for example, maintain their own version of deafening noise (which contributes to their felt arousal levels) with hooters, firecrackers and non-stop drumming.

Novelty and away games

In English soccer, unlike sport in general and soccer in the United States (Roadburg 1980: 271), a tradition has evolved which involves large numbers of fans (and hooligans) travelling to support their team at away matches. This kind of exploratory activity, in which there is a sense of the unknown and of experiencing something novel and unexpected, is considered to be another aspect of the soccer experience or 'atmosphere' that can generate excitement. These emotional feelings are often apparent from interviews with the fans themselves:

> It's like an outing, the feeling of actually being on the terraces with a lot of people with a common aim in their minds, apart from violence, to help the team to win, to see the goals go in and to see a good game. At away games then it's a feeling of actually being somewhere new, of sharing and looking at the other team's ground.
>
> (Marsh 1982: 251).

> Supporting is an expensive hobby, especially for the hundreds of United fans from outside Manchester who have to travel even for the home matches ... But they all thought it well worth it: 'It's a day out', 'There's nothing else to spend our money on round our way', 'You go to places you've never seen before'.
>
> (Harrison 1974: 692–3)

This experience is not limited to travel within the boundaries of England but, when possible, includes international travel to European club tournament or England international matches. The financial outlay involved is seen as an investment for England and 'roughing it' abroad can add to the fun (Williams *et al.* 1984): 'Being a football fan, though, this doesn't matter, for roughing it on your travels is part of the fun. Watching football and the excitement generated at venues all around the world is great' (Ward 1989: 163).

Soccer fan attire

Soccer fans who wear coloured scarves or hats, who carry or wrap themselves in flags or banners, or who paint their faces or other parts of their bodies with team colours, bring opposing qualities together that are likely to produce arousing effects. In the same way that an actor playing a role in a film is at the same time both the actor and the person in real life, so the fan who 'dresses up' is, let's say, both 'our Jimmy' and a Manchester United fan. Remove the make-up, scarf, hat and flag and the fan, after the game, like the actor after the show, becomes the real person again. In this section, the emphasis is on the real–apparent nature of fans' attire. There are other forms of contrasting arousing effects associated with the soccer match, which have not yet been discussed. For instance, Apter (1982: 155) points out that the context (e.g. the physical surroundings, the routine preliminaries to the game, the referee and the strict rules of the game), which is more or less the same week in and week out, provides a degree of security and safety. By way of contrast, the content of the event (e.g. the uncertain outcome and the risk and unexpectedness of the action in the game) has contrasting properties that contribute to the arousing effects. Nick Hornby (1992: 199), a lifelong Arsenal supporter, pointed out the thrill of seeing someone do something that can only be done three or four times in a whole game if you are lucky, not at all if you are not. And I love the pace of it, its lack of formula; and I love the way that small men can destroy big men (watch Beardsley against Adams) in a way that they can't in other contact sports, and the way that the best team does not necessarily win.

The point is that the various forms of contrasting or opposite characteristics found in the soccer context contribute to increases in arousal actively sought by those in attendance.

Empathy with the team

Professional soccer teams, over the period of a soccer season or seasons, face the challenge of playing opposing teams on a regular basis. This is a fundamental characteristic of competitive sport. The highly committed support that is given to a particular team, part and parcel of being a soccer fan, means that the fan is caught up in the outcome, the successes and failures, of the challenges faced by the team (Pearton 1986: 79–80). That fans identify or empathize with players, teams and the feelings associated with their success or failure has been documented by Robins (1984: 96). The challenge of a forthcoming match is arousing for the team, but also for the fans who support the team. The importance of the game, for example a 'top of the table' league decider, provides added significance, thus increasing arousal levels even more. If, after all the anticipation and excitement has been built up, the resulting game proves to be a disappointment, perhaps one side wins too easily, then even the successful team and fans feel let down.

Crowd movement

There are a number of differences between spectator behaviour at professional soccer and at other sports in England. One of these differences concerns the large amount of movement that was possible among fans standing on English soccer terraces. The fact that movement was possible meant that 'surges' in the crowd, the sudden forward movement of large numbers of fans when a goal was scored, for example, became commonplace. Inglis (1990: 25) described these surges very well:

Surging forward, falling backwards, we formed a human roller-coaster, impelled this way and that by a press of bodies, with no need to say 'Sorry' because that was the price you paid for being there. If you didn't like it, then go and sit with the toffs in the stand. We lost our footing, sometimes we lost our heads, but we never lost our sense of theatre. We were the occasion, never forget that. Without us, football would have been a dance to the music of mime.

As history has proved, crowd surges can be dangerous, if not deadly. However, as the quote above illustrates, being caught up in one is an exhilarating experience and provided the person involved perceives it as a safe and secure experience (in a protective frame) it is yet another means of enhancing excitement. However, this source of excitement will not be available to soccer spectators in future. Recent government legislation has forced soccer clubs to change standing terraces to seated areas and old-style crowd surges on the terraces will no longer be possible.

In addition to the strategies used by the regular fan or supporter, there are other strategies that are deliberately used by soccer hooligans to increase arousal and excitement further.

Soccer hooligan strategies

At a relatively innocent level, perhaps, travelling by train to away games without paying was part of the challenge for some of the fourteen- and fifteen-year-old hooligans (Robins 1984: 49). In this case, the challenge was provided by sneaking on and off trains at major London stations, avoiding ticket collectors by climbing over fences, running through the gates, hiding in the toilets on trains or sometimes simply threatening railway ticket collectors.

Other strategies, somewhat less innocent or potentially more harmful in that they are designed to precipitate trouble, include the hooligan 'welcoming committees' that are organized and often wait to ambush visiting fans or hooligans at coach and railway stations (Murray 1977: 9), or attempts to steal rival supporters' scarves, hats or flags (Ward 1989: 16). However, one of biggest sources of challenge to the soccer hooligan is the fun and excitement that can be provided in avoiding apprehension by the police.

Police escorts

The problem of controlling travelling groups of hooligans and preventing them from rioting and wrecking has become a regular one for the police (e.g. Taylor 1982: 158; Ward 1989: 144). For the police it has often been difficult to separate soccer hooligans from the thousands of regular supporters who travel to away games. The police adopted and developed a strategy of containment. It became common practice for visiting 'fans' to be met at the train station and escorted to the soccer ground in groups surrounded by police, some mounted, some with police dogs. At the ground, visiting 'supporters' were, and still are, made to enter through different entrances from the home fans and separated from them by high metal fences, often with a police 'no man's land' in between (Harrison 1974). After the game, a similar procedure occurred and police attempted to escort visiting 'fans' back to the train station. This special treatment – the large police presence, the fact that mounted police and dog handlers are necessary, that the groups are kept together in large clumps and that, as they are marched along, traffic is stopped or diverted, that local people generally avoid the area or, if they live in the vicinity of the soccer ground, board up their houses or shops – can add to the feelings of self-importance and excitement associated with travelling away.

Buford (1991: 42), among a group of English 'supporters' in Turin being escorted by the police in buses to the soccer stadium, recorded his observations:

> A police escort is an exhilarating thing. I felt it to be exhilarating. I didn't particularly like the idea that I did, but I couldn't deny that I was sharing something of the experience of those around me, who, their shouting momentarily muted by the deafening sound, now felt themselves to be special people. After all, who is given a police escort? Prime ministers, presidents, the Pope – *and* English football supporters. By the time the buses reached the city – although there was little traffic, the sirens had been turned on the moment we left the parking lot – the status of their occupants had been enlarged immeasurably.

Soccer hooligan dress

In this connection, it is interesting that Marsh (1978a: 71) should refer to Cameron's (1976) work *Circus factions; blues and greens at Rome and Byzantium*. In the Byzantine Empire, during the fourth century, rival groups of spectators (the blues and greens) began to cause serious problems at the sports spectacles of that time. Apparently, this trouble began when groups of theatre 'rowdies' transferred their allegiance from the theatre, a highly unruly affair, to the circus and its chariot races. Marsh makes, and expands on, the link between these 'classical' hooligans and modern day soccer hooligans. Among the points he makes is one about distinctive forms of dress. The blues and greens wore different coloured sleeves on their tunics so that when they raised their arms in allegiance, in much the same way as contemporary soccer fans with their scarves and flags, these emblems could be seen throughout the hippodrome.

> On the afternoon of the England v Belgium game, several thousand English fans massed together at the station and marched on the stadium. Lots of them looked and sounded pretty fearsome: brawny lads, stripped to the waist, bedecked in union jacks, chanting and shouting. A few loyalist skins among them had shaved union jacks over their shorn heads, and one even had the union jack painted like war paint, over his face.
>
> (Weir 1980: 319)

The word 'skins' used by Weir in the quotation above refers to a sub-cultural youth group, the 'skinheads', who were first seen in the East End of London in 1968 (Clarke 1973). Soon after, they were present in large numbers at soccer games and became the police's and the media's stereotypical image of the violent soccer hooligan (Taylor 1982). Clarke (1973: 12) describes the typical skinhead 'uniform' as

> . . . large working boots, often with steel toe-caps, denim jeans supported by braces, worn with a gap between the top of the boots and the bottom of the jeans, a coloured or patterned, shaped shirt with a button-down collar. Over this was worn a sleeveless pullover and for colder weather a 'Crombie' overcoat. The outfit was topped with very close cropped hair.

He goes on to argue that this highly stylized version of working clothes, which provided a strong sense of identity, was an attempt to recreate the image of the traditional working culture: a reaction to the threat of middle class styles and values epitomized by the 'Mod' styles of the socially mobile white collar worker (Taylor and Wall 1976). In the present context, the skinheads' distinctive dress provides another good example of arousing contrasting effects. In the same way that, when the Manchester United soccer fan described above puts on his soccer 'uniform' for the game, he can take on two identities, so does the skinhead. This latter example, however, is more complex. The skinhead, who was often around fifteen or sixteen years old or younger, 'dressed up' in a way that reflected the tough, mature, traditional British working man. Here, the identity of the youths appeared to be that of the working man, yet clearly in reality it was not. More careful examination reveals that this style of dress parodied the real dress of the working man. The trousers (and hair) were very much shorter than the length associated with the usual image; as a result the heavy boots were wholly visible and the braces, normally covered up, were very much 'on show' over the top of a *smart* shirt. As a result, the identity they were copying was, in a sense, downgraded and exaggerated to such an extent that it became negative. At first, skinheads had a rather ridiculous comic appearance. Later this was to change. 'Everything, the clothes, the haircut, the attitudes and the violence are all overdrawn, as if in self caricature' (Clarke 1973: 16). The aspect that changed was the random unprovoked racial violence, such as 'Paki-bashing' (Williams 1986: 9), by gangs of skinheads that became associated with the comic image described above. This ridiculous or comic image then rapidly became overlaid by threat, malevolence and fear. For the skinheads themselves, this form of negativistic and provocative dressing and the effect it had on others was in itself arousing. Since the advent of the skinheads and their penchant for gratuitous violence, soccer hooligans have been linked to right-wing political groups. This topic is expanded on later in the book.

Avoiding the police

Over the years, hooligans have adopted a whole range of practices that have enabled them to travel to away games and participate in violence and fighting, without being detected prior to the game by the police. For instance, the dress of the skinheads became synonymous with that of the typical soccer hooligan; consequently hooligans began to dress in smart clothes so that they would not be easily recognizable by police. What began as an attempt to foil the police had, by 1985, developed via 'Fred Perry' sports shirts through designer sportswear to 'Armani' and 'Pringle' sweaters (Redhead and McLaughlin 1985). Each individual 'crew' eventually developed its own dress style of upmarket menswear. 'The expensive designer clothes act as individuation as well as camouflage. By wearing Pringle sweaters, the Main Firm were undetectable to police but immediately recognisable to each other.' (Young 1985).

Hooligans also began to avoid the 'football specials': trains organized by British Rail to transport soccer fans to games. On the return journey the train's coaches were inevitably vandalized and wrecked by hooligans enjoying the pleasure of being destructive (see Chapter 3; Ward 1989: 9). In the main, hooligans were by the mid-1980s much better organized, and began to travel incognito on regular public transport or by taking detours via other cities or towns. One innovative scheme, now firmly entrenched in hooligan folklore and well documented in the press (e.g. Young 1985), became the origin of one hooligan group's name, the 'Inter-City Firm'. This scheme, thought up by West Ham's notoriously violent hooligans, involved travelling by expensive first-class Inter-City trains. Their ingenuity allowed them to obtain free first-class rail tickets by taking advantage of a company's promotional offer, which consisted of free rail travel vouchers on the reverse side of washing powder packets. Young (1985: 41) explained the rationale behind the strategy as hooligans responded to the challenge of outwitting the police:

> As well as stressing their prowess, the smart, expensive clothes that the unofficial supporters wear have a practical purpose. By not travelling up in the official transport specially laid on by the clubs, and by looking like the sort of people you'd like to have at your wedding, they avoid the usual anti-hooligan paraphernalia organised by the authorities. They don't have to travel in the police escort, they don't get searched on their way in, and they don't have to sit in the specially allocated sections.

The examples described above illustrate how soccer hooligans enjoy the challenges that are presented by the authorities. Accepting challenges is in itself arousing and even more so if there is an element of danger associated with the challenge. In the same way that people who voluntarily participate in sports such as rock climbing, parachuting or motorcycle racing are deliberately seeking excitement, so are those hooligans who actively search out dangerous situations in and around soccer matches. This strategy for increasing arousal is expanded on in the next section.

Hooligan charges

Hooligan charges became routine occurrences among a range of soccer hooligan activities and became associated in the late 1960s and early 1970s with 'taking an end' (Ward 1989: 8). As Hornby (1992: 55) stated, 'At Highbury they mostly took place on the Clock End, where the opposition's fans stood; usually they were brief flurries, Arsenal fans charging into the enemy, the enemy scattering, the police taking control. These were ritualistic charges, the violence usually contained more in the movement than in the fists and boots.' Taking an end usually involved some degree of prior planning to coordinate infiltration into the 'home end'; when numbers were large enough the violence and fighting began. Murray (1977: 10–11) described how a group of visiting hooligans successfully 'took an end' at a second division game in Manchester.

> About 60 or 70 visiting supporters had infiltrated the home end, and were 'making space' for themselves by attacking supporters. A shout went up from the embankment: '[visiting team's name] aggro'. And a large number of visiting supporters surged down the terracing towards the 4 foot perimeter fence . . . The fence gave way under the pressure, and some 2000 visiting fans ran across the pitch, jumped over the fence at the home end of the ground, and joined their advance commando group.

'Taking ends' or ambushing rival fans walking to or from soccer grounds (Robins 1984: 58) is of course intended to provoke confrontation and violence. In the hooligans' own words it gives them the opportunity for 'steaming in' or charging, which in the soccer context can be seen as a deliberate act on behalf of the hooligans to court danger. Whether this danger is as real as some hooligans perceive is of course a matter for debate (Marsh 1978a). There are, however, enough acts of actual violence and real injury to give those concerned at least the perception of danger, and that, of course, is all that is required for the situation to be highly arousing for the participants. According to reversal theory, however, there are some special features of the soccer hooligan environment which enhance this experience. Protective frames allow people to enjoy danger (see Chapter 2). Through feelings of confidence built up through experience, dangerous activities of many kinds can be experienced as intensely exciting. Given the real potential for serious injury and death, the soccer hooligan environment in and around soccer games is a relatively safe one. In general, the chances of being seriously injured are, realistically, quite small. Consequently, reversal theory argues that much of what goes on in soccer hooliganism is undertaken in the paratelic state, within a protective frame, allowing hooligans the opportunity to intensify their experiences during hooligan aggro.

There are obvious links between reversal theory's concept of paratelic protective frames and Marsh's (1978a) ideas about ritualistic aggro described in Chapter 1. The generation of excitement and danger by hooligans is constrained by the hooligans' own social rules, what have been termed in this book their 'rules of engagement'. These unwritten, but generally well understood, rules permit violence, but only up to a point: it must not be allowed to spoil the hooligan game. Consequently, feelings of fear (usually an unpleasant telic experience) induced by the apparent danger of hooligan confrontation can be experienced as 'parapathic fear' within a protective frame, created by the hooligans' own social rules. High levels of felt arousal accompanying parapathic fear are thus now experienced as pleasant, rather than unpleasant. Incidentally, those watching hooligan fighting, from another part of the stadium or at home on television, would, according to reversal theory, also be doing so in a protective frame.

Occasionally, events occur that may 'break' the protective frame. A good example of this is provided by the tragedy that occurred at Heysel Stadium in Brussels in 1985 when Liverpool played Juventus in the European Cup Final ('t Hart and Pijnenburg 1988). Before the soccer match actually started, thirty-nine people, mostly Juventus fans, died and many others were injured when a retaining wall suddenly crumbled after a 'charge' by Liverpool hooligans. Such accidents are likely to cause an immediate reversal to the telic state in those present, and for some people the trauma is so great that they can never enjoy the soccer experience again. For everyone concerned, hooligans, spectators, police, television commentators and viewers watching television at home, their paratelic protective frames had been shattered. What had begun as exciting, pleasant paratelic feelings in anticipation of the sports spectacle to come, became an anxious, unpleasant telic experience as the circumstances of the tragedy unfolded.

For others, the impact of disasters such as Heysel does not last for long. Soccer hooligan fighting began to recur at other grounds in England a short time after the 'crush' that resulted in ninety-five deaths among Liverpool fans at Hillsborough in Sheffield in 1989. For the fighting hooligans, the protective frame was likely to have been disrupted only temporarily, if at all, and for them the excitement of danger (perhaps even enhanced by their knowledge of the accidents) was still sought within a protective frame.

Soccer hooligan folklore

Anyone who has read an exciting thriller or watched a horror film at the cinema utilizes parapathic emotions for enjoying high arousal. By empathizing with the character or hero figure involved, it is possible to experience vicarious high felt arousal (parapathic experience) without the anxiety or distress (telic experience) that the hero or heroine may be experiencing. In a similar way, soccer hooligan folklore can act as a source of stimulation through the experience of parapathic emotions.

A large amount of interview or self-report material has been collected by observers and researchers since academic interest in soccer hooliganism began in the late 1960s. In many of the scripts, apparently exaggerated accounts of soccer hooligan violence and fighting can be found. Some writers have commented on this and Marsh (e.g. 1978b: 73) especially talks about a 'conspiracy' among soccer hooligans. He states: 'Events must be exaggerated – they must become larger than life. Bloody murder may never happen but there must be at least some foundation for its anticipation.' This is, of course, fundamental to the central thesis of Marsh's (1978a) arguments: that soccer-related aggro is an illusion of violence. His illustrative example clearly underlines the point:

> Question: What do you do when you 'put the boot in'?
> *Fan A:*   Well, you kicks 'em in the 'ead don't you – heavy boots with metal toe-caps an' that.
> Q: What happens then?
>   (puzzled look from fans)
> Q: Well what happens to the guy you've kicked?
> *Fan A:*   He's dead.
> *Fan B:*   Nah! He's alright – usually anyway.
>
>   (Marsh 1978b: 73)

Williams *et al.* (1984: 82–3), in their book *Hooligans Abroad*, reported on participant observation research of English hooligans in Spain during the 1982 World Cup finals, and underlined the importance to the hooligans of conversations about the various reputations of rival hooligan groups and past confrontations (see also Ingram 1985: 54). What the research also revealed was that, on this international trip, hooligans from rival clubs who had joined forces to support the English team had often been on opposing sides during incidents described in these conversations. Such accounts of terrace fighting were subject to differing interpretations, with success and victory being claimed by both sides.

Another example, which shows clearly how a character's reputation is exaggerated and built up as part of hooligan folklore, was given by Ward (1989: 176):

> One character who was certainly larger than life was Hickey. He was known at every football ground in the country and his reputation secured him folk-hero status. Once at Bristol he was confronted by a gorilla of a man who wanted to punch him in the head.
> 'I'm looking for Hickey, Chelsea's leader.'
> 'Well, you've found him.'
> 'Don't be silly, you can't be Hickey. He's big and hard.'
> His reputation had preceded him, and this was to prove his undoing. He loved to play the game of terrace fighting.

Ward went on to point out that because of Hickey's reputation, 'people liked to be seen with him; if he said hello to you it gave you credibility.'

At one extreme, the empathy that people feel towards these 'hooligan heroes' or hooligan gangs can lead to an enhancement of arousal. These feelings may come from merely hearing or recounting stories about the hooligan characters and past exploits of the gangs, such as the 'F-Troop' from Chelsea or the Millwall 'Bushwackers'. At the other extreme, feelings of empathy may also increase on seeing these so-called 'hardmen' and 'fighting crews' going into action.

Hooligan negativism

Being negativistic can enhance high arousal and add to excitement. Negativism is an ingredient in almost all the hooligan strategies described above (Kerr 1988). Two different types of negativism have been identified (McDermott, 1988a, b). The first of these, labelled proactive negativism, is concerned with rebellious or negativistic behaviour for 'the hell of it'. It is hedonistic and gratuitous, engaged in purely for fun and excitement. The second type, termed reactive negativism, often takes the form of vengeful or vindictive behaviour. Reactive negativism, as the name suggests, usually occurs as a reaction to an interpersonal disappointment, 'put down' or insult. In the soccer context much negativistic behaviour is to do with being provocative and deliberately breaking rules. The crowd chants, which include insults and taunts aimed at the police, are one example. Robins (1984: 134–5) describes how police sorties into the crowd to arrest fighting hooligans were accompanied by chants of 'Kill, kill, kill the Bill!' Some of these chants were extremely provocative, as in the case of a chant about Harry Roberts who, after a period 'on the run', was arrested and eventually sentenced to life imprisonment for the murder of two police officers in 1968.

> Harry Roberts is our friend
> He kills coppers
> Put him on the streets again
> Let him kill some others
> Harry Roberts is our friend
> HE KILLS COPPERS!
>
> (Robins 1984: 135)

Negativistic behaviour is not limited to chants. Taken further, negativistic behaviour can result in direct violent confrontation with the police of the sort that occurred on 11 May 1985 at the Birmingham City ground. At half-time, rival groups of Birmingham City and Leeds United hooligans invaded the pitch. Police formed a double cordon across the pitch and, during subsequent clashes, were bombarded with missiles, including bricks, coins, boards and advertising hoardings. Police baton charges were then necessary to restore order on the pitch.

Melnick (1986) makes the point that such efforts to control hooligan deviance may in reality become counter-productive and actually bring about an increase in violence. This is a position shared by Ingham (1978), in agreement with Cohen's (1972) deviance amplification model (or violence amplification model as it was described in Chapter 1) and also in line with reversal theory arguments. Apter and Smith (1976: 27) argue that defying the authorities is often a deliberate attempt by adolescents to gain excitement. 'High arousal in such cases is due to a number of factors including attention, danger, competition and uncertainty of outcome.' Consequently, in these types of situation, increased attempts at control by the police and authorities will only serve to make the environment more attractive to those hooligans seeking excitement and thus probably lead to an escalation of violent confrontation. Proactive negativistic behaviour (just for 'the hell of it') may be changed to or combined with reactive negativism (reaction to disappointment, frustration or personal affront) as hooligans react to police measures, thus causing further escalations in violence and increased attempts at control by the police. The ongoing confrontation between the police and soccer hooligans is further examined in Chapter 6.

Closing comments

In this chapter, which explores a number of strategies that soccer fans and soccer hooligans have for pursuing excitement, it has not been possible to include all the available material. Only examples to illustrate each strategy are given. Furthermore, as the reader may have deduced, some of the examples could have been referred to in connection with more than one strategy. Strategies were separated out merely for convenience and there is an obvious overlap between most of them. Indeed, where overlap does occur it often acts in an additive way to increase or maintain the high levels of arousal that are crucial to the hooligan experience.

It may be of interest to conclude with a quote from a former soccer hooligan, which adds anecdotal support to the main thrust of reversal theory arguments in this chapter. The former soccer hooligan, now a university graduate, began as a seventeen-year-old and spent two years from 1969 to 1971 heavily involved in soccer hooliganism.

> The short answer is that it was fun. As to why, that involves a whole complex of factors of both individual and group psychology, best summed up by saying that it met my emotional needs . . . the excitement of battle, the danger, the heightened activity of body and mind as the adrenaline raced, the fear and the triumph of overcoming it . . . To this day, when trouble starts at a game I come alive and close to getting involved. I may not forget the dangers of physical injury and criminal proceedings but I do ignore them. And yet in other circumstances when I see an argument, even without violence, I feel physically sick.
>
> (Taylor 1984)

Taylor's hooligan 'career' was not affected by the risk of being injured or of being caught and punished. In fact, during this time he was convicted for assault, carrying an offensive weapon and conduct likely to cause a breach of the peace. This did not stop him. It was precisely these elements that contributed to his excitement and pleasure and provided him with the opportunity for paratelic risk-taking behaviour. His experience of the same circumstances away from the protective frame of the soccer situation resulted in a completely different set of unpleasant feelings.

Negativism is possibly the most important strategy for heightening arousal among soccer hooligans. Indeed, the topic is so important that the next chapter will examine negativistic behaviour in much more detail.

References

Apter, M. J. (1982). *The Experience of Motivation: The Theory of Psychological Reversals*. London: Academic Press.

Apter, M. J. (1991). 'A structural phenomenology of play', in J. H. Kerr and M. J. Apter (eds) *Adult Play: a Reversal Theory Approach*. Amsterdam: Swets and Zeitlinger, pp. 13–29.

Apter, M. J. and Smith, K. C. P. (1976). 'Negativism in adolescence'. *The Counsellor*, **23/24**, 25–30.

Buford, B. (1991). *Among the Thugs*. London: Secker & Warburg.

Cameron, A. (1976). *Circus Factions; Blues and Greens at Rome and Byzantium*. Oxford: Clarendon Press.

Clarke J. (1973). 'Football hooliganism and the skinheads'. Occasional paper, Centre for Contemporary Cultural Studies, University of Birmingham.

Cohen, S. (1972). *Folk Devils and Moral Panics*. Oxford: Blackwell.

Harrison, P. (1974). 'Soccer's tribal wars'. *New Society*, 5 September, 692–4.

Hornby, N. (1992). *Fever pitch*. London: Victor Gollancz.

Ingham, R. (1978). *Football Hooliganism: the Wider Context*. London: Inter-action Imprint.

Inglis, S. (1990). 'Farewell to the terraces'. *Weekend Guardian*, 3 February, 24–5.

Ingram, R. (1985). 'The psychology of the crowd – a social psychological analysis of British football "hooliganism" '. *Medicine, Science and the Law*, **25**(1), 53–8.

Kerr, J. H. (1988). 'Soccer hooliganism and the search for excitement', in M. J. Apter, J. H. Kerr and M. P. Cowles (eds) *Progress in Reversal Theory*. Amsterdam: Elsevier, pp. 223–30.

McDermott, M. R. (1988a). 'Measuring rebelliousness: the development of the negativism dominance scale', in M. J. Apter, J. H. Kerr and M. P. Cowles (eds) *Progress in Reversal Theory*. Amsterdam: Elsevier, pp. 297–312.

McDermott, M. R. (1988b). 'Recognising rebelliousness: the ecological validity of the negativism dominance scale', in M. J. Apter, J. H. Kerr and M. P. Cowles (eds) *Progress in Reversal Theory*. Amsterdam: Elsevier.

Marsh, P. (1978a). *Aggro: the Illusion of Violence*. London: Dent.

Marsh, P. (1978b). 'Life and careers on the soccer terraces', in R. Ingham (ed.) *Football Hooliganism: the Wider Context*. London: Inter-action Imprint, pp. 61–81.

Marsh, P. (1982). 'Social order on the British soccer terraces'. *International Journal of Social Science*, **34**, 247–51.

Melnick, M. J. (1986). 'The mythology of football hooliganism: a closer look at the British experience'. *International Review for the Sociology of Sport*, 21(1), 1–19.

Morris, D. (1981). *The Soccer Tribe*. London: Jonathan Cape.

Murray, C. (1977). 'The soccer hooligans' honour system'. *New Society*, 6 October, 9–11.

Pearton, R. (1986). 'Violence in sport and the special case of soccer hooliganism in the United Kingdom', in R. C. Rees and A. W. Miracle (eds) *Sport and Social Theory*. Champaign, IL: Human Kinetics.

Redhead, S. and McLaughlin, E. (1985). 'Soccer's style wars'. *New Society*, 16 August.

Roadburg, A. (1980). 'Factors precipitating fan violence: a comparison of professional soccer in Britain and North America'. *British Journal of Sociology*, 31(2), 265–76.

Robins, D. (1984). *We Hate Humans*. Harmondsworth: Penguin.

Taylor, E. (1984). 'I was a soccer hooligan – Class of 64'. *Guardian*, 28 March.

Taylor, I. (1982). 'On the sports violence question: soccer hooliganism revisited', in J. Hargreaves (ed.) *Sport, Culture and Society*. London: Routledge and Kegan Paul.

Taylor, I. and Wall, D. (1976). 'Beyond the skinheads: some notes on the emergence of Glamrock Cult', in G. Mungham and G. Pearson (eds) *Working Class Youth Cultures*. London: Routledge and Kegan Paul.

't Hart, P. and Pijnenburg, B. (1988). *Het Heizeldrama: rampzalig organiseren en kritieke beslissingen* (*The Heysel Drama: Disastrous Organization and Crucial Decisions*). Alpen aan den Rijn: Samson.

Thayer, R. E. (1989). *The Biopsychology of Mood and Arousal*. Oxford: Oxford University Press.

Ward, C. (1989). *Steaming in*. London: Simon and Schuster.

Weir, S. (1980). 'The sewer rats'. *New Society*, August, 319–20.

Williams, J. (1986). 'White riots: the English football fan abroad', in A. Tomlinson and G. Whannel (eds) *Off the Ball*. London: Pluto Press.

Williams, J., Dunning, E. and Murphy, P. (1984). *Hooligans Abroad: the behaviour and Control of English Fans in Continental Europe*. London: Routledge and Kegan Paul.

Young, T. (1985). 'Saturday afternoon fever'. *The Observer*, 2 June, 41.

5

HOSTILE CONFRONTATION: SOCCER HOOLIGANS VERSUS THE POLICE

Some of the innovative ways that soccer hooligans found to avoid police attempts to control them when travelling to away games were examined in Chapter 4. While these activities were included in the category of generating excitement by accepting a challenge, they clearly also involve elements of negativism. It may be apparent to the reader that being negativistic serves a number of functions for people, especially if those concerned are adolescents or young adults (Apter and Smith 1976). For instance, being negativistic allows the young person to gain a degree of psychological independence from parents, teachers or other authority figures. It may also be seen as an attempt at attention-seeking, and the wide coverage that soccer hooliganism receives from television and the press may well provide reinforcement for future acts of hooliganism.

One of the most important functions of negativism in soccer hooliganism is to gain excitement. This is especially true for situations in which the negativistic state and the paratelic state are combined as paratelic-negativism. When these two states are operative in a person, the real purpose of behaviour is to increase the level of excitement and generally add to the intensity of experience. However, also important in all these examples of rebellious or negativistic acts is the notion of 'felt negativism' (defined in reversal theory as the degree to which one sees oneself behaving in a negative way). High levels of felt negativism contribute to feelings of pleasure and satisfaction in the negativistic state and are likely to be accompanied by a feeling of release. Should the behaviour be provocative enough to spark reaction or retaliation from the police then, provided a reversal does not take place, experienced pleasure and felt arousal will be increased even more (see Figure 5.1).

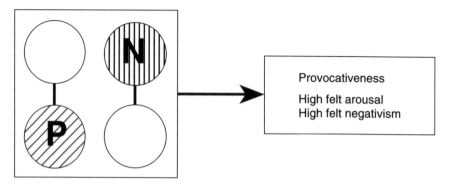

Figure 5.1 A graphical representation of the paratelic-negativism state combination, which leads to a feeling of provocativeness.

The pleasure of being negativistic

According to Reimer (1981: 39) the fact that deviant or rebellious behaviour is often a spontaneous, hedonistic, 'just for the hell of it', fun activity has often been ignored by the work of social scientists. However, studies of rebelliousness and deviance in the workplace underline the fun motive behind many of these activities. Apart from Reimer's (1978) own study, which showed that construction workers regularly take part in stealing, loafing around, drinking alcohol and 'girl watching', as a relief from the boredom of their work, Taylor and Walton (1971) have also recorded a series of examples of what they term 'sabotage as fun'. These include: catering staff on board ship throwing dirty dishes through an open porthole rather than washing them (Ramsey 1966); car workers deliberately placing a banana skin or loose nuts and bolts into sealed parts of a car body, thus sabotaging their own product (Swados 1960); aeroplane factory workers deliberately using tools and methods for fixing wings to the fuselage that are prohibited by management (Bensamn and Gerver 1963); and the half mile of Blackpool rock that had to be destroyed because the usual pattern running its length had somehow been replaced by the words 'fuck off' (Challinor 1969). It is not only studies of rebelliousness in the workplace that illustrate the pleasure of being negativistic. There are, in addition, a number of examples of research work on delinquency in young people that support this view (e.g. Gibbons 1965; Ferdinand 1966; Cohen 1973; Donnermeyer and Phillips 1984; Jones and Heskin 1988).

The observation that social scientists have failed to take account of the spontaneous, hedonistic nature of rebellious and negativistic acts cannot be levelled at reversal theory (e.g. Jones 1981). Indeed, this notion has played a central role in the reversal theory explanation of negativistic behaviour (Apter 1982: 203), which has subsequently been supported by reversal theory research (see McDermott 1986, 1988a, b).

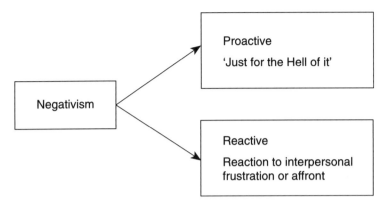

Figure 5.2 The two types of negativism.

Negativism and rebelliousness in young people

McDermott's (1988a, b) research included several British and American male and female university and high school student samples and used both psychometric and interview techniques. Following statistical analysis of the psychometric data, two types of negativism were identified. These were labelled 'proactive negativism' and 'reactive negativism' (see Figure 5.2). Proactive negativism was found to be related (in males, for example) to poor psychological health and arousal seeking, while reactive negativism was found to be positively associated (in the American high school students, for example) with non-excused absences from school and school referrals, and negatively associated with grade point average scores.

The interviews with young people furnished a rich supply of supportive material, including this response from a subject who was asked how he felt about doing what he knew he should not have done:

> Not at all guilty. Actually it gave me great pleasure going out. I suppose I enjoy doing things I know I shouldn't be, or, say I can't afford to do something so I'll do it. Well I think I spoil myself sometimes and just go out. I enjoy things better if I'm not supposed to do them than if I am supposed to do them or if it's o.k. to do them, because I get more excitement out of doing them then. 'Course you're a bit guilty about it but that was o.k., that was. I wasn't bothered at all.
>
> (McDermott 1988b: 322)

This quotation is clearly about proactive negativism. Another subject, who answered the same question by saying she went to a party instead of revising for an exam, was asked how she felt about that, and gave an answer that has elements of both proactive and reactive negativism. She replied:

Well, I'm not bothered to revise at the moment, 'cause I don't give a shit about exams, so I didn't mind at all. I've always thought that way. I just don't have any respect for some reason. I've always walked out of exams. I've always done it. I don't know why. I just think there are better things I should be worrying myself about and better things to be doing.

(McDermott 1988b: 320)

Two other research studies provided observational and interview evidence that supports the view of negativism put forward by reversal theorists. The first of these, carried out by Corrigan (1979), was an ethnographic study of the life experience of working class youth in Sunderland, a city in the north-east of England. The second was undertaken by Welsh (1981), who completed an eight-month participant observation study of adolescents of mixed age, sex and race living in Bethnal Green, a traditionally working class area of London. Both writers point out that adolescents from these areas tended to avoid the relatively restricted, structured leisure venues like the youth club, and spent much of their leisure time hanging around the streets 'doing nothing' or waiting for something to happen.

Saturday evenings were spent, for a whole variety of reasons, on the street. Once on the street the boys seemed to engage in a series of activities which they labelled as 'doing nothing'. Whilst 'doing nothing' some of them would have 'weird ideas'; and on many occasions a weird idea would get them into trouble.

(Corrigan 1979: 121)

Welsh's (1981) study indicates that alternative venues for leisure activities, such as youth clubs, cannot compete with the attractiveness of the street, with its freedom from parental or adult supervision and the discipline of work or school.

And the street provides a unique blend of risk and safety. To go out on the street is to put yourself at risk. Many of the risks are mundane, such as being run over, but some are less routine, such as the possibility of becoming involved in a fight or in confrontation with a powerful authority, notably the police. The most extreme element of risk is that involved in delinquency. If delinquency is attractive then the street must be attractive for it is the obvious setting for many delinquencies. Yet the street also provides safety. There is the safety of anonymity. One can abuse policemen, throw stones at cats, annoy motorists and so on with very little risk of any comeback.

(Welsh 1981: 259)

Thus, not only does the street provide a potential source of proactive, 'just for the hell of it', negativism through the manufacture of excitement, it is also potentially rich in opportunities for reactive negativistic acts during interaction with the police or other forms of authority. Welsh also describes how the risk activities of the street are undertaken within what reversal theory would term a protective frame. High levels of felt arousal and excitement are generated in a kind of negativistic game, played within a specially demarcated area, and bound by its own system of rules. Rival groups of adolescents, residents, shopkeepers and the police all vie for control (either real or symbolic) of this demarcated area of public space, the street. Consequently, the potential for confrontation, for playing the 'game', for generating excitement, is almost unlimited. In this game the most exciting confrontations, because they carry the greatest risk, are with the police and are therefore most frequent (Welsh 1981).

In many ways, looking for trouble at soccer matches is really an extension of the experience created and structured by youth on the street (Corrigan 1979). When an individual is being negativistic, there are thought to be three related phenomenological components of the behaviour (Apter 1982: 198). Of importance here are the meaning and interpretation that the person gives to his or her own negativistic behaviour (Cohen 1972: 13; Apter 1982: 202). These are known as the source, the requirement and the desire to act against the requirement. Consider, for example, the case of a regular soccer supporter wanting to travel to another city to watch a soccer match. The *source* may be announcements from the government and soccer authorities that they are going to 'clamp down' on future acts of soccer hooliganism. On the day of the match the police, who are hostile and unfriendly as a response to the announcement, organize very tight control over the supporters, 'requiring' them to be escorted from the station to the soccer ground where they (and other visiting fans) are placed in an enclosure bounded by metal fencing. As a result the soccer supporter, now feeling extremely negativistic, may, for example, feel 'compelled to act against' this control by breaking out of the enclosure or making things as difficult as possible for the police escort. The supporter may even join the hooligans among the crowd by attacking police horses or causing other kinds of trouble on the way back to the train station after the match. In this way, police measures designed to prevent disturbances may actually provoke trouble.

The police at work

The very essence of police work would appear to be telic in orientation. Burglaries, car theft and bank robberies, not to mention muggings, assault and occasionally murder, are criminal activities that have to be dealt with in a serious manner. Counteraction to this type of criminal activity often requires a high degree of planning. Even in carrying out fairly routine duties (even the word duty carries connotations of obligations and seriousness), such as directing traffic, the police are generally serious and professional about their work. Apart from obvious examples, like driving at speed during emergency calls or in car chases (Holdaway 1977), there are not too many aspects of police work, at least at face value, which could be described as likely to be paratelic in orientation. Despite the telic oriented nature of their work, individual police officers, just like other workers (Walters *et al.* 1982), will reverse between telic and paratelic and between the other pairs of states as they carry out their duties. For instance, when giving someone directions, giving talks to children in schools or passing on bad news to relatives of someone killed or injured in a car accident, they are likely to be in the sympathy metamotivational state. At other times, such as when interviewing suspects after a crime or dealing with speeding drivers, they are much more likely to be in the mastery metamotivational state.

However, it seems that when they are in the paratelic state, under typical working conditions of 'long periods of quiet interspersed by brief moments of action' (see Cain 1973; Holdaway 1977), they, like soccer hooligans and delinquents, are likely to be bored. Consequently, they may, on occasion, take whatever opportunities are available to manufacture excitement in an effort to counteract boredom (Welsh 1981). Several research studies carried out on the police have highlighted the provocative nature of police operations with adolescents. A number of different reasons have been put forward by researchers to explain why this occurs. For example, police boredom has been suggested by Robins and Cohen (1978) as one of the reasons why they sometimes provoke youths into doing something foolish, so that they can then take action. Making an arrest may be the easiest way to manufacture some paratelic action and excitement and to counteract boredom.

Attempts to counteract the disrespectful attitude of a particular group of adolescents towards the police is thought by Welsh (1981; see also Tauber 1967) to be a more valid reason for police harassment of juveniles than boredom. In reversal theory terms, this can be seen as the police in the mastery state attempting to counter the negativistic attitude of the adolescents. Holdaway (1977) has pointed out that some police officers enjoyed the financial rewards accruing from overtime at soccer matches, and some police arrests at soccer matches were made to allow the police officers concerned to fiddle overtime by spending extra time at the law courts, a practice which Holdaway (1977) said was at least partially sanctioned by supervisory officers. This particular behaviour would appear to be rooted in the autic (perhaps in combination with the negativistic) metamotivational state(s).

While there may be some officers who would be deliberately provocative or enjoy 'snatching' hooligans from a soccer crowd and arresting them, it seems more than likely that the majority of the police carrying out their duties at soccer grounds can generally be categorized as being in a telic-conformist-alloic state combination. Controlling or attempting to control the behaviour of soccer hooligans would almost certainly mean that the police will also be in the mastery state. To summarize, the police are likely to be experiencing a combination of telic, conformist, alloic and mastery metamotivational states (see Figure 5.3).

Hooligans   Police

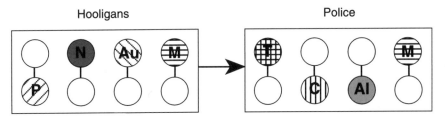

Figure 5.3 The different operative metamotivational state combinations for soccer hooligans and the police.

Police operations with soccer supporters

It has already been established that soccer fans are more than likely to be in the paratelic state, given the fact that they are about to watch or are watching an exciting spectator sport. The average or regular fan will, however, also be in the conformist state: following police directions to the ground, buying a ticket, going to his or her designated area in the soccer ground and so on. The soccer hooligan, in contrast, will probably be in a paratelic-negativistic metamotivational state combination and, as has been described, might well engage in a number of activities from which negativistic pleasure can be gained. What can be said about fans and hooligans with respect to the mastery–sympathy and autic–alloic pairs of states?

Among fellow fans who want their team to win and the rival team (and accompanying supporters) to lose, the soccer fan will probably be in an alloic-mastery state combination. In these circumstances with this state combination operative, the team comes first, not the supporter. The supporter identifies with a particular team and powerful feelings are often induced by the team's success or failure during the natural ebb and flow of the game. Should the team win, the fan will probably experience a pleasant feeling of pride; should the team lose, the fan's experience will probably be one of humiliation. The overall motivational state combination for the fan is one of paratelic-conformist-alloic-mastery and the transactional emotions, pride and humiliation are often experienced by fans.

Police operations with soccer hooligans

The hooligan's feelings are different from those of the fan. The soccer hooligan is concerned with winning, causing rival hooligans to run from the hooligan 'rucks', being involved in fighting with the police and avoiding arrest, and generally gaining status among his peers. Most of the time during the action he is concerned with himself. As a result, a combination of paratelic, negativistic, autic and mastery states is likely to be the overall metamotivational arrangement for the soccer hooligan (see Figure 5.3).

It should be apparent that the police and the soccer hooligans are experiencing a number of opposite metamotivational states (the police are telic-conformist-alloic; the hooligans are paratelic-negativistic-autic), which undoubtedly will lead to different interpretations of events. In addition, both groups are likely to be in the mastery state. However, as far as the police are concerned, their state of mastery is flavoured by autic-telic-conformity and their experience will be very different from that of the hooligans, whose state of mastery is coloured by autic-paratelic-negativism. Hence there is every likelihood that a struggle for mastery will occur, with each group attempting to gain and maintain the upper hand from completely different metamotivational foundations. For the hooligans it is fun and excitement and a kind of game (Marsh 1978; Apter 1992) and for the police it is a serious matter of controlling a threat to public order and individual safety, a part of their duty:

> Those responsible for law and order, as one can discover if one studies the development of football, have again and again fought bitterly against the upsurge in excitement in people and particularly of communal excitement, as a grave social disturbance. The pleasurable excitement people experience in relation to mimetic events thus represents a social enclave where excitement can be enjoyed without its socially and personally dangerous implications. That it is often enjoyed in the company of others enhances the enjoyment.
>
> (Elias and Dunning 1970: 50)

It is wrong to suggest that the metamotivational state combinations in Figure 5.3 will always be present in hooligans and police. Reversals can and do take place. The terrible tragedy at Hillsborough in 1989 when ninety-five people were killed in a crowd 'crush' provides a good example of this. A late surge of fans rushing into one particular section of the fenced areas or 'pens' on the terracing, already full to capacity, caused the injury and death of many of the fans trapped at the front against the fence. After a period of confusion and chaos, fans and police eventually worked together to help the victims. There was, however, a long delay on the part of the police, who did not at first realize, or refused to accept, that fans were in definite danger and were attempting to escape injury or death, rather than attempting a pitch invasion. The delay by the police may have been due to the fact that their operational metamotivational state combination is very heavily influenced by telic-mastery and individual police officers failed to reverse to the sympathy state until they understood the real nature of the terrible (contingent) event taking place. McIlvanney (1989) wrote, 'Perhaps it is understandable that policemen go to football matches these days with their thoughts concentrated on keeping hostile mobs at bay rather than on supervising the safety of a mass audience. But that predisposition carries the seeds of deadly consequences.'

In an interview by Chappell (1987) with a twenty-year-old London-based Manchester United supporter, and his friend, a Millwall supporter, this telic mastery-oriented approach by the police is demonstrated. What is more, these supporters, without realizing it, even suggest a more effective approach, which in reversal theory would be termed a paratelic-sympathy-oriented approach.

Peter says the police don't understand the minds of football supporters. 'Most fans were brought up in working class areas where you don't take any shit from anyone.' Derek suggests a bit more good humour from the boys in blue, and less of the hair-trigger reaction to anyone taking the piss out of them. 'Don't get us wrong, you've got to respect the police for the job they do. With football they are just not going about it the right way.'

The police and authorities as amplifiers of soccer hooligan activities

Some writers (e.g. Taylor 1971; Dunning *et al.* 1982) have expressed the view that traditional soccer support has been formed by rough working class sub-cultures in which violence was an intrinsic component. In addition, there has been a long history of animosity between the working class, and the forces of law and order. Pearson (1983: 86) stated:

> . . . in many working class neighbourhoods hostility towards the police was a remarkably cohesive force. Typically sparked off by what might have been seen as an unfair arrest or an arbitrary use of police power, resistance to arrest on this scale was such an entirely common feature of working-class life before the Great War that it constitutes the most articulate demolition of the myths of deep-rooted popular respect for law and authority in England.

There are a number of documented examples in the literature that concentrate on forms of deviancy, such as drug use and gang fights between Mods and Rockers (e.g. Cohen 1972). At least two of these examples focus on working class youth and on a working class community. The police, magistrates and other control agents, by their attempts to restrict or limit these activities, can, paradoxically, amplify the deviant behaviour of those involved. Furthermore, there are sufficient examples from the literature on soccer hooliganism to illustrate how the process of deviancy amplification and violence amplification (see Chapter 1) can occur in the soccer context.

Let us first briefly examine how the amplification process has worked in other situations involving deviant behaviour and then, second, focus in on soccer hooliganism. Young (1971), for example, described how the police and the system of drug control in operation in the late 1960s in the Notting Hill area of London actually acted in such a way as to amplify the deviant behaviour of the drug user. Building on the ideas of Wilkins (1965) and the results of his participant observation research, Young (1971) identified a series of ongoing changes on the part of the police and drug users that resulted in amplification of the deviant behaviour. The police decide to act against the drug users. Interpretation of the police action by the drug users is followed by an adaptive response. This, in turn, leads to a different police action against a changed group and yet another more extreme adaptive response to the changing situation from the drug users. Again the police respond by undertaking different and increasingly severe actions towards the changed group. In this way, a seemingly unending spiral of deviancy amplification develops (Wilkins 1965).

Cohen (1972) describes how police action in dealing with gang fights between Mods and Rockers tended to affect or even stimulate subsequent delinquent behaviour. During the early stages the police affected the youths' behaviour in two ways. The police tactic of 'moving along' youths harmlessly hanging about at police-designated 'trouble spots' illustrated how police action tended first to provoke immediate angry responses from the youths and, second, in a more sustained fashion, to involve the police in 'making the rules whose infraction constituted deviance' (Cohen 1972: 166). The result was that the police spent a good deal of their efforts enforcing these rules and attempting to maintain respect while doing so (see also Becker 1963). The results of this action were, as Cohen points out, counterproductive:

> The more sustained effects of police action were less visible, but, in terms of the amplification model, as important. These effects were to increase the deviance by unwittingly solidifying the amorphous crowd forces into more viable groups for engaging in violence and by further polarizing the deviants against the community.
>
> (Cohen 1972: 169)

In passing, it should be noted that there is a basic difference between the reversal theory approach to deviance and sociological explanations of deviant behaviour (e.g. Cohen 1972). Being negativistic is, from the perspective of reversal theory, something that is phenomenological in nature and therefore based on the interpretations of individuals themselves, not on judgements by an external group (Apter 1982). Consequently, in reversal theory people are only being negativistic if they perceive themselves to be so. Note, though, that people may well be influenced by the views of others in assessing whether their actions are indeed negativistic. This is clearly a different view from the sociological view of deviance taken by Cohen, for example, where society marks a group as deviant. In spite of this conceptual difference, the notion of a spiral of amplification of negativism (and/ or soccer hooligan violence) is still relevant in reversal theory and is explained below.

There is more recent evidence which suggests that police action may paradoxically amplify negativistic behaviour. For example, Hoyland (1989) gives an account of a West Midlands police drugs raid in Wolverhampton.

As a result of the raid, in which 120 officers 'swamped' a public house and local witnesses accused police of beating up or arresting innocent people, gangs of youths rioted, looted shops, set fire to council offices and stoned firemen. Wolverhampton's senior community relations officer was reported as saying, 'The scale of the police operation could be to blame for the way it escalated' (Hoyland 1989).

Similar sentiments in the context of soccer hooliganism have been expressed by Taylor (1971). According to Taylor, a process of amplification of deviance, similar to that described by Cohen (1972), occurred with regard to the degree of social control applied to soccer, which only added to the problem. Taylor (1971) argues that, as the scale of social control increased (for example, stiffer sentences for soccer hooligans and the increased willingness of the police to arrest hooligan offenders), the number of hooligan offenders appearing in the crime statistics increased. To the authorities, the need for further control was thus underlined, but as new initiatives were taken they tended to unify the ranks of soccer hooligans into renewed and more extreme acts of violent resistance.

> The reaction of Liverpool supporters was directed not towards the Sheffield goal but rather to the over-reaction of plain-clothes mob squads to traditional displays of defiance (the collective raising of 'V' signs). The intervention of the mob squad and the hordes of uniformed officers at the Liverpool end of the ground resulted in the most determined and collective aggressive resistance I have ever witnessed on a football league ground.
>
> (Taylor 1971: 160–1)

Taylor was writing some twenty years ago; since that time attempts at intervention by the police and the authorities have increased even more. For example:

1 An increase in the scale of judicial punishment given to individual soccer hooligan offenders, with repeated calls from politicians and others for even tougher sentences.
2 Action by the European football authorities (UEFA), banning English clubs playing in Europe following the Heysel Stadium disaster in 1985.
3 Increasing attempts by police at control, including: separating rival groups at matches in pens surrounded by spiked fences; closed circuit television crowd surveillance techniques; proposals for a national membership authority and the use of identity card schemes (the Luton Town club have implemented their own membership card scheme, which bars visiting soccer fans from their ground); soccer hooligan group infiltration through police undercover operations and the formation of a National Football Intelligence Unit with computerized data banks on known soccer hooligans.
4 A number of additional governmental inquiries, reports and recommendations following the Heysel Stadium disaster in Belgium (1985), the Bradford City fire disaster (1985) and the Hillsborough disaster (1989).

When the authorities or the police take tougher measures to make it more difficult for the hooligans, the hooligans themselves perceive the situation as being more interesting and challenging. Thus, measures intended as a deterrent paradoxically only add to the pleasant hooligan experience of very high levels of felt arousal and felt negativism, thus further amplifying and reinforcing the behaviour in a similar manner to that described by Cohen (1971) and Taylor (1971). Buford (1991) illustrates how these more recent measures, especially those involving the police, have escalated soccer hooligan violence:

> Steve blamed most of the current troubles on the police. 'The police have now got it so good,' he said, 'that we're more constrained than before. We just don't have the time that we used to have. The moment a fight starts we're immediately surrounded by dogs and horses. That's why everyone has started using knives. I suppose it might sound stupid but because the policing has got so good we've got to the point where we have to inflict the greatest possible damage in the least amount of time, and the knife is the most efficient instrument for a quick injury. In fact the knifings – because there is so little time – have become quite symbolic. When someone gets knifed, it amounts to an important victory to the side that has done the knifing. If the policing was not so good I'm sure the knifings would stop.'
>
> (Buford 1991: 120–1)

Closing comments

Any discussion about police operations with fans and soccer hooligans must concern itself especially with the negativism–conformity pair of metamotivational states. Regular fans can enjoy the match without being a problem to the police and others because the conformist state is operative, thus keeping their paratelic experience within certain confines. This is not true for soccer hooligans, as the negativistic state strongly influences their behaviour. Indeed, their overall operative metamotivational state combination is diametrically opposed to that of the police and is an almost certain recipe for conflict.

It should be apparent why measures taken by the authorities and the police are largely ineffective in stopping soccer hooligan violence. It seems that each and every measure taken to prevent trouble proves to be counter-productive and acts in a way that stimulates and provokes renewed violence. There are strong psychological forces at work here and the reinforcement of negativistic hooligan acts spirals to more and more extreme levels. Brown's (1991a, b) research work with gamblers provides a useful parallel for understanding this behaviour and his Hedonic Tone Management Model of addictions and its application to soccer hooliganism is closely examined in Chapter 7.

This piecing together of the different operative metamotivational state combinations for supporters, hooligans and police has begun the process of discovering the answers to some of the fundamental questions posed in Chapter 1. In the next chapter, the same approach will be used to examine aspects of the conflict and fighting between hooligan gangs that have not previously been discussed in detail.

References

Apter, M. J. (1982). *The Experience of Motivation*. London and New York: Academic Press.

Apter, M. J. (1992). *The Dangerous Edge*. New York: Free Press.

Apter, M. J. and Smith, K. C. P. (1976). 'Negativism in adolescence'. *The Counsellor*, **23/24**, 25–30.

Becker, H. S. (1963). *Outsiders: Studies in the Sociology of Deviance*. New York: Free Press.

Bensamn, J. and Gerver, I. (1963). 'Crime and punishment in the factory: the function of deviancy in maintaining the social system'. *American Sociological Review*, **28**, 588–98.

Brown, R. I. F. (1991a). 'Gaming, gambling and other addictive play', in J. H. Kerr and M. J. Apter (eds) *Adult Play*. Amsterdam: Swets and Zeitlinger, pp. 101–18.

Brown, R. I. F. (1991b). 'Mood management, self states as goals and addiction models of criminal behaviour'. Paper presented at the British Psychological Society Division of Criminal and Legal Psychology and Department of Psychology, Rampton Hospital Conference, *Addicted to Crime*, Nottingham, March.

Buford, B. (1991). *Among the Thugs*. London: Secker and Warburg.

Cain, M. (1973). *Society and the Policeman's Role*. London: Routledge and Kegan Paul.

Challinor, R. (1969). *Socialist Worker*, 22 April.

Chappell, H. (1987). 'When tempers rise on the terraces'. *Guardian*, 26 August.

Cohen, S. (1972). *Folk Devils and Moral Panics: the Creation of the Mods and Rockers*. Oxford: Blackwell.

Cohen, S. (1973). 'Property destruction: motives and meanings', in C. Ward (ed.) *Vandalism*. New York: Van Nostrand Reinhold, pp. 41–51.

Corrigan, P. (1979). *Schooling the Smash Street Kids*. London: Macmillan.

Donnermeyer, J. F. and Phillips, G. H. (1984). 'Rural vandalism in the USA', in C. Levy-Leboyer (ed.) *Vandalism: Behaviour and Motivations*. Amsterdam: North-Holland.

Dunning, E. G., Maguire, J. A., Murphy, P. J. and Williams, J. M. (1982). 'The social roots of football hooligan violence'. *Leisure Studies*, **1**(2), 139–56.

Elias, N. and Dunning, E. (1970). 'The quest for excitement in unexciting societies', in G. Luschen (ed.) *A Cross-cultural Analysis of Sport and Games*. Champaign, IL: Stipes, pp. 31–51.

Ferdinand, T. N. (1966). *Typologies of Delinquency: a Critical Analysis*. New York: Random House.

Gibbons, D. C. (1965). *Changing the Law Breaker: the Treatment of Delinquents and Criminals*. Englewood Cliffs, NJ: Prentice-Hall.

Holdaway, S. (1977). 'Changes in urban policing'. *British Journal of Sociology*, 28(2), 119–37.

Hoyland, P. (1989). 'Police accused over drugs raid riot'. *Guardian*, 25 May, 2,

Jones, R. (1981). 'Reversals, delinquency and fun'. *European Journal of Humanistic Psychology*, 9(5), 237–40.

Jones, R. S. P. and Heskin, K. J. (1988). 'Towards a functional analysis of delinquent behaviour: a pilot study'. *Counselling Psychology Quarterly*, 1(1), 35–42.

McDermott, M. R. (1986). 'Rebelliousness in adolescence and young adulthood: a two dimensional model'. Paper presented at the Annual Conference of the British Psychological Society, City University, London, December.

McDermott, M. R. (1988a). 'Measuring rebelliousness: the development of the negativism dominance scale', in M. J. Apter, J. H. Kerr and M. P. Cowles (eds) *Progress in Reversal Theory*. Amsterdam: Elsevier, pp. 297–312.

McDermott, M. R. (1988b). 'Recognising rebelliousness: the ecological validity of the negativism dominance scale', in M. J. Apter, J. H. Kerr and M. P. Cowles (eds) *Progress in Reversal Theory*. Amsterdam: Elsevier, pp. 313–25.

McIlvanney, H. (1989). 'The lost tribes'. *The Observer*, 23 April, 13.

Marsh, P. (1978). *Aggro: the Illusion of Violence*. London: Dent and Sons Ltd.

Pearson, G. (1983). Hooligan: a History of Respectable Fears. London: Macmillan.

Ramsey, R. A. (1966). *Managers and Men: Adventures in Industry*. Sydney: Ure Smith.

Reimer, J. W. (1978). 'Deviance as fun – a case of building construction workers at work', in K. Henry (ed.) *Social Problems – Institutional and Interpersonal Perspectives*. Glenview, IL: Scott Foresman, pp. 322–32.

Reimer, J. W. (1981). 'Deviance as fun'. *Adolescence*, 16, 39–43.

Robins, D. and Cohen, P. (1978). *Knuckle Sandwich*. Harmondsworth: Penguin.

Swados, H. (1960). 'The myth of the happy worker', in M. Stein, A. Vidich and D. M. White (eds) *Identity and Anxiety*. New York: The Free Press.

Tauber, R. K. (1967). 'Changes in urban policing'. *Issues in Criminology*, 3(1), 69–81.

Taylor, I. R. (1971). 'Soccer consciousness and soccer hooliganism', in S. Cohen (ed.) *Images of Deviance*. Harmondsworth: Penguin, pp. 134–64.

Taylor, L. and Walton, P. (1971). 'Industrial sabotage: motives and meanings', in S. Cohen (ed.) *Images of Deviance*. Harmondsworth: Penguin, pp. 219–45.

Walters, J., Apter, M. J. and Svebak, S. (1982). 'Colour preference, arousal and the theory of psychological reversals'. *Motivation and Emotion*, 6(3), 193–215.

Welsh, S. (1981). 'The manufacture of excitement in police–juvenile encounters'. *British Journal of Criminology*, 21(3), 257–67.

Wilkins, L. (1965). 'Some sociological factors in drug addiction control', in D. Wilner and G. Kassebaum (eds) *Narcotics*. New York: McGraw-Hill.

Young, J. (1971). 'The role of the police as amplifiers of deviancy, negotiators of reality and translators of fantasy', in S. Cohen (ed.) *Images of Deviance*. Harmondsworth: Penguin, pp. 27–61.

6

VIOLENT ASSAULT: HOOLIGANS VERSUS HOOLIGANS

Throughout this book, numerous examples have been given and references made to hostile and violent incidents between hooligan gangs and their rivals. In Chapter 4, for example, some of the strategies used by hooligans to enhance their experience during fighting were described. There are, however, some aspects of soccer hooligan violence that have not previously been discussed in detail, and these will be covered here.

In Chapter 1, an alignment with a particular team was described as being a kind of flag of convenience under which soccer hooligans could perpetrate aggressive and violent acts. The competition or struggle that the hooligan is involved in has less to do with the soccer team and more to do with bands of hooligans accompanying the rival team. With individuals in any hooligan gang likely to be in the mastery state, there is a struggle to gain mastery over their hooligan opponents (also in the mastery state) in any confrontation that might take place. At one level, the struggle involves attempts to gain mastery over another group through, for example, chanting and singing insults, and, at another level, through 'taking ends', fighting and ambushing rival hooligan groups at railway stations.

This chapter will focus on the latter more violent aspects of soccer hooliganism. Important here are the mastery and autic metamotivational states. When people are in the mastery state they generally want to feel tough and strong and perceive the situation they are in as a competition or struggle; people in the autic state are concerned principally with what happens to them during interactions with others.

There are plenty of examples that illustrate the desire for mastery and concern with oneself among hooligans:

> This time the Italians backed off only a short distance. We held our ground at the top of the steps. They advanced slowly but surely, throwing cans and bits of bottle . . . I spotted a young Italian about

twenty years old wearing a leather jacket; he seemed to be some kind of leader, so I decided he was the one for me. A roar went up, and down the steps we went into the mass of Italians. I felt the crunch of flesh and bone as my bit of wood hit a skull. The Italians retreated and a large body of Arsenal fans chased them along the terraces, whacking them on their backs and kicking them up the backsides.

(Ward 1989: 79)

Another notorious example from soccer hooligan folklore involved leaving business or calling cards with the victims at the scene of a hooligan 'ruck'. These cards, in one case of expensive vellum and gold-embossed, carried messages that said, for example, 'Nothing personal – you have been serviced by the Anti-Personnel Firm' (Young 1985), 'You have been nominated and dealt with by the Chelsea Head Hunters' (Keel 1987) or 'Government health warning. Leeds fans can seriously damage your health' (Davies 1986). Such acts, while they could be seen as adding to the 'game' by leaving a possible clue for the police, also emphasize one hooligan group's mastery over another and add to its notoriety.

As mentioned in Chapter 5, the hooligans' overall metamotivational state pattern is one of autic-mastery combined with paratelic-negativism. Thus, in the soccer situation, with rival gangs of hooligans in opposition, individuals in both groups are likely to be experiencing a metamotivational state combination of paratelic-negativistic-autic-mastery. This state combination forms the general basis for many of their hooligan activities. However, during hostilities, only a minor change in these operative metamotivational states is needed to alter the individual hooligan's emotional experience and lead to the development of real aggression and anger. This change is explained in the following section.

Aggression, anger and arousal

Aggression is behaviour that has the deliberate intent of causing physical or psychological injury to another person. However, a kind of playful 'paratelic aggression' can occur in the absence of anger and is often engaged in deliberately to create interesting and exciting situations. Many forms of sport are characterized by paratelic aggression in which aggression and counter-aggression occur as an intrinsic element of the competitive sports process. This is certainly so in the case of professional soccer, where the whole atmosphere in the soccer stadium is permeated with provocative aggression. This is true not only of the players competing on the field, but also of the spectators in the stands. At the same time, soccer hooligans add to this basic layer of paratelic aggression by building on their own more extreme forms of provocative paratelic aggression. The feeling experienced by the hooligan in this type of situation is best described as 'provocativeness' and has accompanying high levels of felt arousal and felt negativism (see Chapter 5). The aggressive behaviour is therefore

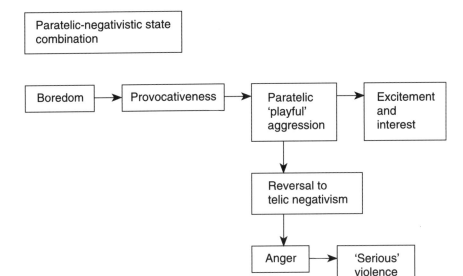

Figure 6.1 A graphical representation of the development of anger and 'serious' violence during soccer hooligan activity.

paratelic but also heavily overlaid with negativism in a powerful combination of the two metamotivational states as paratelic-negativism. Here the goal of the behaviour is to precipitate a response from rival hooligans. Should the rival group not respond, this may induce increased feelings of boredom, which may then in turn lead to more extreme acts of provocative aggression in order to produce the desired level of arousal and excitement (see Figure 6.1). Should a reversal take place, from the paratelic to the telic metamotivational state, then the high levels of felt arousal that accompanied the hooligan's provocative behaviour will be changed. The underlying metamotivational state combination will then become telic-negativism, but will still be accompanied by high felt arousal. The hooligan's overriding emotional experience is now one of anger, an unpleasant emotion.

Anger is a telic-oriented emotion, but the situation is made more complex by the possibility that anger can also be experienced as a parapathic emotion in the paratelic state. (To distinguish between real anger (telic) and parapathic anger (paratelic) the latter form will be placed inside quote marks as 'anger'). Anger does not always lead to aggressive behaviour and neither does 'anger'. However, for hooligans in a paratelic-negativistic state combination, 'anger' is likely to give rise to aggressive behaviour. Situations in which 'anger' can be experienced are also very likely to be actively sought by soccer hooligans and used to maintain and elevate levels of felt arousal and felt negativism even further.

Consider a typical scenario. Outside the soccer stadium soccer hooligans often direct their aggression against other people. For example, Saturday shoppers in a busy high street suddenly faced by the approach of a group of aggressive, rampaging soccer hooligans are, if there is time, likely to flee from the situation. However, if a rival group of hooligans should attempt to retaliate against the hooligans' aggression then there are two possible outcomes. Increased feelings of aggression and 'anger' can bring about an escalation of the situation and violent confrontation will occur, especially if a reversal takes place and paratelic-negativistic (parapathic) 'anger' becomes anger (telic-oriented). On the other hand, if the retaliatory response is sufficiently severe, the original pleasant experience may reverse to one of telic-oriented fear and may result in them running away (see Buford 1991: 306). However, even feelings of fear in these situations can be enjoyed if the protective frame is not broken and the hooligan's fear can be experienced as paratelic-oriented parapathic 'fear'.

Reversals that might induce an emotional change from pleasant parapathic 'anger' to anger are thought to take place quite rapidly and, as with the other metamotivational states, to be induced by contingent events, frustration or satiation. In the typical soccer environment there are certainly plenty of opportunities for contingent events (e.g. a particularly vicious attack by rival hooligans) or frustration (failure of their team to achieve the desired result) to induce reversals in individual or even groups of soccer hooligans. In comparison with most other games, soccer is a particularly frustrating game since scoring is so infrequent. Examples of reversals arising as the result of satiation are perhaps less obvious, but hooligans who have been on the rampage for a long period of time (perhaps before, during and after the match) may eventually reverse due to the effects of satiation. There are, however, numerous examples of hooligan riots at soccer games as a result of frustration, including Manchester City fans whose team lost their chances of promotion at Notts County (6 May 1985), and Leeds United hooligans whose team failed to win against Birmingham City at St Andrews and were therefore unable to join them in promotion to the first division. One example described in the Danish press (*Ekstra Bladet* 23 September 1982), where it seems likely that both frustration and contingent events led to violent attacks by hooligans, occurred in Copenhagen during Denmark's game with England in 1982:

> But the worst incident came when Jesper Olsen equalised for Denmark. About 500 English fans stood up ready to fight, knowing that the victory had been snatched.
> A group of Danish fans didn't help when they threw beer bottles at their heads. The English reaction was to shout, 'England! England! England!' and to go for Danish fans with the English specialty, kicking with boots, about 15 of them kicking one Dane. Later it spread to the whole of Osterbro. About 50 hooligans were arrested.
>
> (Williams *et al.* 1984: 165)

To summarize, then, the behaviour of soccer hooligans who, for example, travel away to soccer matches and break windows and destroy cars (Foster and Road 1985) comes from paratelic-negativism. The excitement and pleasure that hooligans achieve from provoking 'aggro' with foreign hooligans (Williams 1986) also comes from paratelic-negativism, but once the fighting actually starts, the source of the hooligans' pleasant experience will probably change from excitement to parapathic 'anger', experienced within a protective frame.

Soccer hooligans and extreme right-wing political groups

Adolescents who, for example, grow their hair long or wear banned clothing or jewellery as a negativistic response to parents' or school rules, are at the same time often conforming to the 'rules' or accepted values of their own adolescent subculture:

> ... behaviour which appears from the outside to be negativistic, and is classified as deviant, may well be performed in a conformist state of mind. Teenage vandals or student 'dropouts' may well feel themselves to be conforming to norms, these being derived from subcultures different to the subcultures of those people who define the behaviour as deviant, and they may even be unaware that they are acting against certain requirements. Reversal theory argues nevertheless that deviant behaviour *may* be chosen as a deliberate rejection of society's requirements, and suggests that often, if not always, deviant behaviour *does* have such negativistic origins.
>
> (Apter 1982: 203–4).

Kaplan (1984) has suggested that there are two possible sources of satisfaction that can be achieved by becoming part of such subcultures. He argues that sources of individual satisfaction may come from the attractiveness of a group that, for example, considers delinquent behaviour as appropriate, in addition to the pleasure the individual may achieve by carrying out such acts.

Conforming to the subcultural norms of the group and becoming accepted by the group may also provide a source of satisfaction for the soccer hooligan. For example, in 1968, many soccer hooligans adopted the codes of behaviour and dress of the notorious skinheads who first came to prominence in London's East End and began to turn up in considerable numbers at soccer matches all over England (Clarke 1973). As was mentioned in Chapter 4, the skinheads, with their reputation for unprovoked racial violence (both inside and outside the soccer context) (Carr 1987), became the stereotypical image of the soccer hooligan of that time. The racist element in soccer probably started with the advent of the skinheads, and there has always been a strong suggestion of links between soccer hooliganism in England and extreme right-wing political groups like the National Front (e.g. Price 1981; Robins 1984; Williams *et al.* 1984; Ward 1989):

> The hard-man, though, lives in a more dangerous and unchanging world. Permanently sensitized to 'trouble' in his environment, his paranoid fantasies about defending his 'patch' against outsiders make him ripe for manipulation by the politics of the extreme right. At Millwall, during the 1977 season, out of a home gate of 3,500, some two hundred young men were sighted standing shoulder to shoulder in para-military uniform, displaying the insignia of the National Front and of the British Movement.
>
> (Robins 1984: 110)

In Italy, soccer hooliganism has been linked with both left-wing (at Milan and Bologna) and right-wing (at Lazio, Ascoli and Verona) groups (Roversi 1991), although Williams (1986) had claimed previously that in Milan the highly organized gangs were fascist, as were those in Turin and Rome. According to Van Limbergen *et al.*, (1987), hooligans in Belgium and Holland, like their English counterparts, have definite links with extreme right-wing organizations. After the Brussels Heysel Stadium tragedy, newspapers carried photographs of the many Nazi and neo-fascist emblems among the crowd. Before the recent reunification of Germany, the activities of the 'Borussia front', a neo-Nazi group based in Dortmund who prompted fighting at soccer matches, and other groups in Hamburg, Munich and Frankfurt were known to the authorities (Williams 1986).

The fascist presence at soccer games in England, described by Robins (1984), was previously noted by Price (1981: 12) who attended a match between West Ham and Sheffield Wednesday, played at Upton Park, West Ham's home ground. 'The *ambiance* was nauseating – a sea of dirty denim emblazoned with union jack and swastika, imitation Heil Hitler salutes, pounding violence in the verbal obscenities, menace in patches of the home crowd on its way home.'

Certainly, in England, there have been numerous racist incidents at soccer matches, and in some cases black players have had to put up with constant barracking from the crowd. In 1994 there are, perhaps, some signs that things are slowly changing, but a similar claim about diminishing numbers of racist incidents in soccer was also made by Price in 1981, six years before the incidents described here. One episode was a particularly good example of the racial bigotry that is characteristic of English soccer crowds. In 1987, John Barnes, one of the most talented attacking players in England at the time, was transferred to Liverpool from Watford. Liverpool had been the most consistently successful club in English soccer for over twenty-five years, but had never had a black player who could establish himself permanently in the team. John Barnes is black. When he played his first match against local rivals Everton, every time he touched the ball he was booed. Everton's fans chanted 'Everton are white' and when he came

near the touchline people swore at him and threw bananas on to the pitch
(Hill 1989). Barracking black players was not limited to club matches;
there were also incidents at England international matches. When England
played Denmark in September 1982, black England players were booed
and jeered when they touched the ball (Williams *et al.* 1984: 149); When
England played against Turkey in Istanbul in 1984, hooligans made mon-
key noises and threw bananas at black England players (Ward 1989: 154).
In addition to what has happened to black players, black supporters have
been beaten up and driven out of some club grounds (Robins 1984: 114).

In spite of examples like those above, some authors are sceptical about
the level of involvement of right-wing political groups in soccer hooliganism, claiming that there is little hard evidence (Canter *et al.* 1989: 119;
Ward 1989: 179). If these groups are active, however, one question needs
to be answered: do right-wing groups deliberately set out to recruit soccer
hooligans, or are members of right-wing groups attracted to soccer hooliganism because of the opportunity it offers for participating in violence?
According to Robins (1984: 114), a campaign in soccer stadia in 1980, in
which literature and newspapers were handed out, became a priority tactic
in fascist recruitment efforts. Canter *et al.* (1989), however, were of the
opinion that right-wing groups merely cash in on violence in soccer hooliganism, rather than instigate it. In fact, there are probably elements of
truth in both viewpoints. What, however, does reversal theory have to say
about the motivation behind aggressive and violent behaviour of such
groups?

Rather than necessarily being in agreement with or even knowing much
about the politics of the extreme right (Billig and Cochrane, 1981; Canter
et al. 1989), soccer hooligans who join such groups can express their
paratelic negativism even more. Society perceives such groups as deviant,
so they become an attractive proposition for those who want to, for example, 'kick back' against societal constraints. By joining a fascist group,
a soccer hooligan is being negativistic but, paradoxically, at the same time
by taking on the norms and values of that group is being conformist.
However, the negativistic and conformist aspects do not occur at the same
time, they are alternative views. In other words, the group, as perceived
and identified by the individual hooligan, is defined by contrast with an
'outgroup'. The leader (or leaders) of such groups, probably telic-negativistic
for much of the time, are not conformist but will also take on a role where
they are in the autic-mastery metamotivational state combination for much
of the time. By contrast, the members of the group, by means of an alloic-
mastery state combination, can feel strong by being subservient. Here,
paradoxically, the stronger the leader and the weaker and more subservient the members of the group, the stronger they feel. Of course, the leaders
and group members are not in these metamotivational state combinations
all the time and there will certainly be ongoing reversals between the
different pairs of states. What is being conveyed here is the fact that they
are likely to be in these particular metamotivational state combinations for

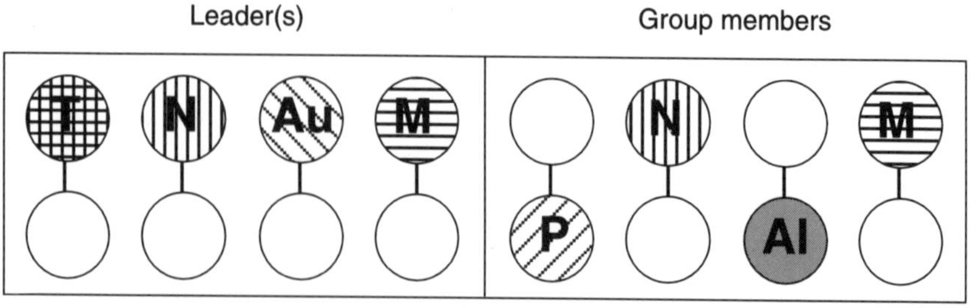

Leader(s)   Group members

Figure 6.2 The different operative metamotivational state combinations for right-wing group leaders and members.

a good deal of the time and especially when engaging in their fascist activities (see Figure 6.2).

Hard core soccer hooligans and extreme right-wing political group members have been involved in 'hate campaigns' and violent attacks against particular racial groups (e.g. Carr 1987). While other emotions, such as resentment, may also have a part to play, and accompanying feelings of perceived unfairness and frustration may add to the intensity of the negativistic behaviour, the net outcome is the likely generation of the highly charged emotional state of anger. Remember that anger is both a negativistic and a high arousal emotion. Therefore, when anger is further combined with high felt negativism, any resulting action is pleasant. Thus, when the hooligans vent their anger by beating people up in these racist attacks, both the moment of the attack itself and the time immediately after will be a highly enjoyable experience (Apter 1989: 102). The importance of the mastery state here should not be forgotten. After all, racial bigotry and violence is entirely about one race or group's mastery over 'inferior' races and peoples. Indeed, the Nazis considered themselves to be 'the Master Race'.

The media and the amplification of soccer hooligan gang violence

Cohen (1972) was quite definite about the influential role of the mass media in their reporting of the incidents between Mods and Rockers in England in the 1960s. He argued that some incidents occurred because of publicity seeking behaviour (a form of excitement seeking) by individuals and groups, which was directly attributable to the way in which the media publicized previous events. Media coverage that focused on the antagonism between Mods and Rockers not only triggered imitation effects, but also transmitted the values and imagery associated with stereotypes from each group, thus making the mobilization of increasing numbers of participants relatively easy. Cohen (1972) also argued that the media magnified the differences between the two groups and gave them a structure and mythology (thus creating increased curiosity and excitement among some observers) that were unjustified at the time and helped further to polarize the deviants against society. 'This led to running battles between the cops and mods. We were encouraged by the press hysteria . . . Or if the news-papers reported that the rockers' bike gangs were going to invade the South Coast resorts we would get all excited and ready to meet 'em' (Robins 1984: 40)

The media's main objective is obviously to maximize sales or the num-bers of people viewing or listening. In order for a news item to have the maximum impact it needs to rate highly in 'news worthiness'. It is there-fore perhaps not surprising that the media tend to hyperbolize the ordinary to make it sound extraordinary, often combining it with the suggestion of unexpectedness and negative consequences (Hall *et al.* 1978). For example, articles in the tabloid papers carry bold headlines and are generally short but contain shocking, sexy or scandalous material which is oriented to a paratelic readership. The reason why so many people buy tabloid news-papers is that, in comparison to more 'serious' (telic-oriented) papers, the tabloids are, for them, much more exciting to read.

The soccer context

Young (1986) examined themes in the mass media following the Brussels Heysel Stadium disaster in May 1985. He found that there was consistent and extensive coverage of the Heysel riot story for four weeks in Britain and North America. However, the press continued to refer to it in relation to other soccer-related hooligan incidents for up to eighteen months after the Brussels disaster. Several recurring themes and modes of representation and style in the press reporting were identified, which, Young (1986) claimed, had an important impact on the way people interpreted and discussed this incident.

> Combined with evocative and inflammatory commentaries regarding blame, 'irrational' and 'animal' behaviour, military rhetoric, the need for violent punishment etc., the cumulative effect of all this was that for some time the dominant 'public voice' became very much centred around an intensified and panic-ridden law-and-order campaign, with the alleged threat offered to the general public by soccer hooliganism quickly gaining momentum.
>
> (Young 1986: 262)

He went on to describe several aspects of the press treatment of soccer-related disorders, which are similar to those outlined by Cohen (1972). The ideas were elegantly illustrated by Buford (see also Ward 1989: 185):

> They were trying to create it: not only were they not stopping the masked, missile throwing Juventus fans, but they were also not photo-graphing them. It was images of the English they wanted.

They wanted the English tattoos; their sweaty torsos, stripped to the waist; their two fingers jabbing the air; the vicious expressions on their faces as they hurled back the objects that had been thrown at them. Italians behaving like hooligans? Unheard of. English behaving like English? *That* was interesting! I remember thinking: if the day becomes more violent, who do you blame? The English whose behaviour on the square could be said to have been so provocative that they deserved whatever they got? The Italians, whose welcome consisted in inflicting injuries upon their visitors? Or can you place some of the blame on these men with their television equipment and their cameras, whose misrepresentative images served only to reinforce what everyone had come to expect.

(Buford 1991: 76–7)

Research evidence on media effects

Gunter (1987), in reviewing the research evidence about television viewing and antisocial and violent behaviour, pointed out that many of the findings are somewhat equivocal. Furthermore, it is difficult to generalize research evidence from laboratory studies, field experiments, correlational studies and panel studies to wider contexts owing to the limitations of the specific research methodologies adopted by researchers. Gunter (1987) argued that what is apparent from the research evidence is that while early violence viewing has not been found to contribute to the development of later aggressiveness (Atkin *et al.* 1979) the effects of viewing television violence appear to be mediated by personality factors. For example, programmes involving violence are sought out and enjoyed by people who exhibit aggressive personality characteristics. The perceptions of physically aggressive individuals were also found to be different from those of less aggressive individuals (Gunter 1983). Physically aggressive individuals found fist fight footage on television more exciting and less disturbing or violent than less aggressive subjects.

It would appear that the relationship between television viewing and the amplification of violence or antisocial behaviour is not a simple cause and effect one, and may be a good deal more complex than the simplistic view often expounded by the authorities and the media themselves.

Soccer hooligans on television

Young people watching images of soccer hooliganism on television will probably experience them as fascinating and perhaps exciting, while adults (or, for example, members of the judiciary or police) watching will experience them as unpleasant and disturbing.

For example, in the 1960s the incompatible characteristics of the contrasting dress and behaviour of Mods and Rockers – short neatly combed hair versus long untidy greasy hair (rockers were also called greasers in some areas); quiet customized scooters versus loud racy powerful motorbikes; a combination of long army combat jackets and smart pressed Levis (not jeans) versus leather and denim – created effects that added to the transmitted images of deviance on television. Going beyond dress and behaviour (see Chapter 4), other contrast effects can be identified in police–hooligan conflict around soccer. The serious work of the police versus the recreational fun and excitement of the hooligan, adults versus young people and adolescents, authority and rules versus rebelliousness, telic conformity versus paratelic negativism, good versus bad in a similar way add to the ambiguity of hooligan situations often seen on television news programmes (Coulson 1991). The outcome is that the intensity of the hooligan viewer's experience is phenomenologically enhanced.

> In the paratelic state the ambiguity may be welcomed and enjoyed. · It sets a puzzle to be solved and increased arousal may be associated with this. It may also enhance the intensity of experience through a · contrast effect between the opposite meanings, especially where these are of the strong variety defined earlier. While ambiguity remains non-threatening, the resulting heightened arousal and experience will therefore be pleasurable.
>
> (Apter 1982: 152)

In the same way that young people may identify with an actor playing a role or a pop star, some viewers may experience feelings of empathy as they identify with soccer hooligans portrayed on television (Apter 1982: 162). Soccer hooligans seeing themselves on television will revel in the fact they are 'on the telly', giving them an increased sense of importance and adding to their status within their own hooligan gangs. The importance of the role of the media in reinforcing violent soccer hooligan activities should not be underestimated. Some of the most violent superthug hooligans, whose activities are described in detail in the next chapter, collected press reports and recorded their escapades in diaries. The importance of the media is underlined by Buford (1990). In describing a soccer hooligan he stated:

> Richard wanted to explain to me what it meant to be a supporter of Manchester United . . . Other people went out of their way to do the same: they wanted me to understand. All day long people stopped me to illustrate, to define, to comment upon the condition of being one of the lads. I cannot remember meeting people so self-conscious about their status and so interested in how it was seen by others. They were members of something exclusive – a club, cult, firm, cultural phenomenon, whatever it might be called – and they valued its exclusivity. They were used to the fact that the world was interested in them and were accustomed to dealing with television and newspaper journalists in a way that few people however educated in media matters, could hope to be.
>
> (Buford 1991: 114)

Closing comments

Paratelic-negativism, provocative aggression and parapathic 'anger' are all key elements in the motivation of soccer hooligans. For the hardened soccer hooligan, appeasement and the flight of the victims are not very useful in maintaining and enhancing even higher levels of arousal, but will probably lead to decreases in their feelings of anger and perhaps even eventually generate boredom. What the hardened soccer hooligan wants is retaliation by members of the public, by the police or by rival gangs of soccer hooligans. In the resulting violent confrontation they can enjoy to the full the 'kick' associated with extreme levels of high arousal and high felt negativism. It is in this way that soccer hooligans become addicted to the experience of high felt arousal associated with violent confrontation and assault. These activities generally only involve hard-core soccer hooligans, the 'superthugs', and they as a special group of individuals are the subject of the next chapter.

This chapter has also attempted to show how soccer hooligans can become attracted to, and involved in, neo-fascist groups that are aggressive and violent towards innocent bystanders who find themselves in the wrong place at the wrong time. In addition, reversal theory explanations of how the methods and approach of the press and other media could contribute to the processes of behaviour reinforcement and the escalation of hooligan violence were given. The motivational jigsaw with respect to soccer hooliganism is nearing completion.

References

Apter, M. J. (1982). *The Experience of Motivation*. London and New York: Academic Press.

Apter, M. J. (1989). *Reversal Theory*. London: Routledge.

Atkin, C., Greenberg, B., Korzenny, F. and McDermott, S. (1979). 'Selective exposure to televised violence'. *Journal of Broadcasting*, **23**, 5–13.

Billig, M. and Cochrane, R. (1981). 'The national front and youth'. *Patterns of Prejudice*, **15**(4), 3–15.

Buford, B. (1991). *Among the Thugs*. London: Secker and Warburg.

Canter, D., Comber, M. and Uzzell, D. (1989). *Football in Its Place*. London: Routledge.

Carr, M. (1987). 'Racism's short fuse'. *The Observer*, 22 November, 49–50.

Clarke J. (1973). 'Football hooliganism and the skinheads'. Occasional paper, Centre for Contemporary Cultural Studies, University of Birmingham.

Cohen, S. (1972). *Folk Devils and Moral Panics: the Creation of the Mods and Rockers*. Oxford: Blackwell.

Coulson, A. S. (1991). 'Cognitive synergy in televised entertainment', in J. H. Kerr and M. J. Apter (eds) *Adult Play: a Reversal Theory Approach*. Amsterdam: Swets and Zeitlinger, pp. 71–85.

Davies, J. (1986). 'Superyob! The new breed of sick hooligan striking fear into our soccer clubs'. *Daily Express*, 12 February.

Foster, J. and Road, A. (1985). 'Fans predicted soccer riot that caught police and BR on the hop'. *The Observer*, 17 March, 4.

Gunter, B. (1983). 'Do aggressive people prefer violent television?' *Bulletin of the British Psychological Society*, 36, 166–8.

Gunter, B. (1987). 'The psychological influences of television', in H. Beloff and A. M. Coleman (eds) *Psychology Survey 6*. Leicester: British Psychological Society, pp. 276–304.

Hall, S., Critcher, C., Jefferson, T., Clarke, J. and Roberts, B. (1978). *Policing the Crisis: Mugging the State, and Law and Order*. London: Macmillan.

Hill, D. (1989). '. . . And the crowd goes bananas'. *The Independent*, 4 March, 27.

Kaplan, H. B. (1984). *Patterns of Juvenile Delinquency*. London: Sage Publications.

Keel, P. (1987). 'Four fans led football violence campaign'. *Guardian*, 9 May, 1.

Price, C. (1981). Football fascism. *The Spectator*, 10 January, 12–13.

Robins, D. (1984). *We Hate Humans*. Harmondsworth: Penguin.

Roversi, A. (1991). 'Football violence in Italy'. *International Review for Sociology of Sport*, 26(4), 311–31.

Van Limbergen, K., Colaers, C. and Walgave, L. (1987). 'Onderzoek naar de maatschappelijke en psycho-sociale achtergronden van het Voetbalvandalisme' ('Research into the social and psychosocial background of football hooliganism'). Katholieke Universiteit Leuven.

Ward, C. (1989). *Steaming in: Journal of a Football Fan*. London: Simon and Schuster.

Williams, J. (1986). 'White riots', in A. Tomlinson and G. Whannel (eds) *Off the Ball*. London: Pluto Press, pp. 5–19.

Williams, J., Dunning, E. and Murphy, P. (1984). *Hooligans Abroad*. London: Routledge and Kegan Paul.

Young, K. (1986). '"The killing field": themes in mass media responses to the Heysel stadium riot'. *International Review of Sociology of Sport*, 21, 253–65.

Young, T. (1985). 'Saturday afternoon fever'. *The Observer*, 2 June, 41–2.

7

HARDMEN, SUPERTHUGS AND PSYCHOPATHS

In almost every book or extensive piece that has been written about soccer hooliganism, considerable attention is given to the ringleaders of soccer hooligan violence. The ringleaders are members of a special category of hooligan to which different writers have given their own different names. Marsh (1978), for example, categorized hooligans into several different groups, including 'aggro leaders' and 'fighters', from the larger hooligan group. Robins (1984: 16) talked about 'hardmen' and Williams *et al.* (1984) about 'hard cases'. Popplewell (1986), in his government report, described the emergence of what he termed the 'new hooligan', while Buford (1991) included a number of descriptions of 'topmen'. Here they will be referred to as 'superthugs'.

'Frankie', a sixteen-year old member of a 'fighting crew', provides a typical description of a superthug called 'Buster' in Robins (1984):

> He's the top man of all the crews, I reckon. He's the best fighter. He's mad, goes around with a shooter or a cut-throat. Any time there's a fight he has to steam in first. He used to have to fight with the top man of the other End. I haven't seen this, I've just heard about it . . . The top geezers in the Kington was a bloke called Micky Spiers, and then there was Stanley Pewter. They was all big blokes. The best fighters. They were a bit older than the other kids. Micky and Stan was mates. They're inside now for somink.
>
> (Robins 1984: 58–9)

Although there is a fairly obvious degree of exaggeration in this quote, it is clear that the younger hooligans, like 'Frankie', were very much in awe of the hooligan leaders. Moreover, it can easily be seen how stories and anecdotes about the hooligan leaders can be built up into a kind of folklore of soccer hooliganism.

The early writers on soccer hooliganism were agreed that most soccer hooligans came from the working class (Corrigan 1977; Dunning *et al.* 1982). Taylor (1976) argued that the roots of soccer hooliganism were to be found in the 'violent masculine style' of the 'rough working class tradition' (see Chapter 1). However, in the mid-1980s Popplewell (1986) suggested that a new type of hooligan had emerged on the soccer scene. These new affluent hooligans, often older and holding down good jobs, dressed smartly and had money to spend on travelling to soccer games 'in style'. Later writers also documented this apparent change in the hooligan leaders from 'hardmen' to 'superthugs'. By way of illustration, Buford (1991) makes much of an intelligent, cultivated, well-educated and well-read, bilingual, Jewish hooligan called DJ.

> In the figure of DJ I had the fundamental contradiction at its most concentrated. He had so many things going for him – education, intelligence, an awareness of the world, money, initiative, a strong and supportive family . . . Implicit in my thinking was the liberal commonplace that those who 'turn against society' – I felt that destroying its property and inflicting injury on its members could be described as 'turning against society' – have been denied access to it. This wasn't true of DJ.
>
> (Buford 1991: 220)

In a sense, this quote brings the discussion right back to the kind of question posed in the first chapter. Why is it that individuals (sometimes educated, financially well-off, and from a 'good background') engage in hooligan activity, when, on the surface at least, there would appear to be no real need to do so? Examining the background and character of these superthugs in more detail might allow an insight into the motivation for soccer hooligan violence to be gained.

The headhunters

Following a five-month police undercover operation at the end of 1985 and the beginning of 1986 involving the successful infiltration of a soccer hooligan gang by six young constables, five of the gang's leaders were brought to trial and prosecuted on 9 May 1987. In typical fashion, details of the activities of the 'Chelsea Headhunters' or, as they were called in some newspapers, the 'Chelsea Mob', were widely reported in the British press after the trial (e.g. the *Daily Telegraph*, the *Guardian*, the *Independent* and *The Times*, all 9 May 1987). From these press reports of the evidence presented in court, several very important features of the hooligan leaders' behaviour became evident and require special mention here.

For instance, the age of the convicted gang leaders ranged from twenty-three to thirty-one, well beyond the teenage years; all four were working and one was a former Royal Navy cook and Falklands War veteran (Tendler 1987). Indeed, journalists seemed surprised that the gang's 'field commander', Terry Last, a slightly built non-drinker, worked as a clerk for a top firm of London lawyers and thus 'hardly fitted the conventional image of the football hooligan as a mindless lout' (Keel 1987a).

In addition, an important feature of the 'Headhunters' hooliganism was the degree of detailed planning invested in setting up opportunities for 'aggro' with rival hooligans, most of it apparently carried out by Last: 'The violence they generated was anything but spontaneous. Between them they could mobilise about 400 hooligans, marshalling them like military commanders to engagements planned weeks, sometimes months in advance' (Darbyshire 1987). For away games, for example, rather than allowing themselves to be apprehended by local police security operations, they would travel out of their way, arriving unexpectedly from a completely different direction at a station in a particular city where trains from London did not stop. This extravagant method of travel was financed from thousands of pounds retained in a number of bank accounts. The gang also planned diversions for police at Chelsea's home ground, Stamford Bridge, which then allowed the main bulk of the 'Headhunters' to charge the visiting supporters.

This type of meticulous planning activity is a telic activity carried out in anticipation of a reversal to the paratelic state. In this case, the telic planning activity is only engaged in to enhance the later paratelic experience. In other words, by planning ahead the gang leader could, for example, avoid the likelihood of the hooligan's paratelic-negatavistic excitement being prevented by police intervention on the way to the soccer stadia before the real action took place. Moreover, for the individual or individuals concerned, planning ahead would, based on their previous experiences, lead to feelings of excitement and anticipation of the violent events to come.

Interestingly, the press (e.g. the *Daily Telegraph*, the *Guardian* and the *Independent*, all 9 May 1987) reported the discovery by the police of a series of diaries (the *Independent* also mentioned a scrapbook) kept by Last, which detailed the gang's hooligan acts. For example, the *Independent* highlights one diary entry by Last for 24 December 1984, when Chelsea travelled to play Newcastle. Serious violence took place and one Newcastle fan was left with horrendous slash wounds across his face, arms and chest. The Newcastle fan subsequently identified Last in court as one of his assailants (Keel 1987b). Last wrote, 'We done a pub load of Geordies. We done well against the Geordies – they were terrified outside the pub' (see Mills 1987). These diary entries went back several years and also recorded acts of violence at England matches abroad, including, for example, after the game on 29 February 1982 when England defeated France in Paris. Chief Superintendent Hedges, who led 'Operation Own Goal', may well have been correct when he stated: 'A lot of these people are fairly insignificant individuals in their ordinary lives. Perhaps it was their way of achieving some glamour and notoriety' (Keel 1987c).

This view would certainly fit in with the reversal theory arguments about paratelic excitement seeking presented earlier in this book. After all,

Last was a clerk in a solicitor's office, a job liable to be telic-oriented and characterized by long periods of low arousal. Furthermore, by keeping a diary, Last would be able to use it to help recollect past events, perhaps reliving some of the excitement and danger again. Indeed, Buford (1991: 282–3) provides some support for this view in his description of a conversation he had with 'Mutton-chops' while in Italy for the World Cup in 1990. Mutton-chops, as Buford called him, was on the British Football Intelligence Unit's list of the top 100 convicted soccer hooligans. During his conversation with Buford, he took out a newspaper cutting in which there was a photograph of himself and an article on how the soccer thugs, in spite of all the police security activity, were still able to arrive in Italy. 'Mutton-chops regarded it as a matter of great prestige to be on the list of one hundred – and of even greater prestige then to slip into Italy' (Buford 1991: 283).

Incidentally, it is interesting to note that later in the same conversation, Mutton-chops mentioned that Terry Last and Stephen Hickmott had both been released early from prison for good behaviour and would be showing up at the match (Buford 1991: 284). Hickmott, or 'Hickey' as he was known among the hooligans (see also Ward 1989: 102), was one of the hooligans convicted with Last following the police undercover operation 'Own Goal'.

Other superthugs

In spite of intensive efforts, not all police undercover activities were successful. At least three trials in 1988 collapsed after forensic scientists cast doubt on police evidence gathered in undercover operations. However, a number have been successful and have led to the conviction of the leaders of several soccer hooligan gangs that were linked to soccer teams in cities across England.

For example, twenty-four members of the 'Cambridge Casuals' were sentenced to between five months and four years in prison after a fight with Chelsea fans in Cambridge in February 1985 (Hardy 1985). Again the planning and organizing ability of the hooligans was evident. Apparently harmless bystanders directed unsuspecting Chelsea supporters to a pub where they were set upon by a gang of hooligans. The leader of eighty 'Casuals', a twenty-five-year-old window cleaner, described by the judge as a 'deliberate organiser of violence', received five years in prison. He had two previous convictions for possessing an offensive weapon and assaulting a police officer. At Leeds Crown Court, five leaders of a hooligan gang known as 'the Para Army' were convicted of conspiring to fight and cause affray during the 1986–7 soccer season (Johnson 1988). The prosecution had alleged that the men, aged from twenty-six to seventeen years, plotted violence against rival fans, blacks and police. On 27 May 1988, four Millwall hooligans, reported to be part of a gang of fifty hooligans who attacked passengers on a train carrying Arsenal and Charlton supporters at New Cross station in London, were jailed for a total of twenty-nine years (*Guardian* 28 June 1988). Their ages ranged from twenty-five to twenty-eight and, in this case, three of the four were unemployed. In passing sentence, the judge spoke of a 'planned and organised affray'. The thirty-year-old leader of the 'South Midland Hit Squad', a hooligan group of 150 members linked to Oxford United soccer club, was jailed for three years after a fight with eighty Queen's Park Rangers fans, which involved bottles, glasses, kicks and punches. The convicted man had three previous convictions for violence (*Guardian* 21 May 1988).

It becomes obvious from the court reports above that the hooligan leaders share a number of common characteristics. They were, for example, extremely good at planning and organizing hooligan episodes. As Superintendent Appleby, head of the National Football Intelligence Unit formed in 1989, stated, 'I think there is organisation and ringleaders. Spontaneous hooliganism occurs a lot less than planned hooliganism. It is purely for the joy of combat, of hurting people' (Sharratt 1989).

While some authors (e.g. Canter *et al.* 1989) remained sceptical about whether there were any real differences between these 'new hooligans' and the older 'hardmen', reviewing the information provided by the court reports above and other sources (e.g. Keating 1985) allows a profile of the superthug to be pieced together.

1 These hooligans are usually in their mid to late twenties, sometimes even more than thirty years old.
2 Their involvement in soccer hooliganism has usually endured since their teenage years.
3 They are not necessarily unemployed and some may even have professional jobs (see above) or be university students (Taylor 1984).
4 They may well be married and be family men with mortgages.
5 They often have previous convictions for violence.
6 They may well exhibit good, often innovative, skills in the organization and planning of hooligan activities.
7 They seldom drink before a game, needing to be alert when 'steaming in'.
8 Some keep a record in the form of a diary or scrapbook.

Several of the points listed above indicate a commitment to soccer violence among the hardcore thugs that goes far beyond that of the 'middle of the road' soccer hooligan. Given the average age and period of involvement in soccer hooliganism, there is also a suggestion here of an ongoing process of hooligan development, which somehow 'grips' some soccer hooligans in their earlier years so that they develop into the superthug types described above. Examining the reports of superthug behaviour and the statements and quotations attributed to them, there would appear to be a strong similarity between the processes involved in developing into a hardcore soccer thug and the processes involved in some forms of addiction. The work of Iain Brown at the University of Glasgow has focused on, for example, gambling addiction, alcohol addiction (e.g. Brown 1988, 1991a) and, more recently, criminal behaviour (Brown 1991b), and may provide an understanding of how superthugs become addicted to soccer violence.

Soccer violence: an addiction

Over the past few years Brown (1991a, b) has outlined the basic propositions of what he terms the Hedonic Tone Management Model of Addictions. This psychological model, which relies heavily on concepts and ideas from reversal theory, shows how addictions, ranging from substance abuse (cocaine, alcohol, tobacco) to non-substance abuse activities (exercise, eating, work), follow the same basic stages in their development. It is a major contention of this book that the hardcore soccer thugs become addicted to soccer-related violence. In the following sections it will be shown, with the aid of Brown's model, how the addictive process begins with early involvement in soccer hooliganism and develops in some cases to the level of violent activity characteristic of the soccer superthugs.

The important relationship between felt arousal and pleasant and unpleasant moods has already been emphasized in this book. People generally develop their own repertoire of techniques for manipulating and modulating, or what might be termed managing, arousal levels. The examples are seemingly almost endless and, although obviously specific to particular individuals, include such mundane things as a stimulating early morning cup of coffee or listening to a relaxing favourite piece of music, going for an exciting night out with a girl or boyfriend or soaking in a hot bath while reading a book. These examples are of the short-term variety; others can be more long-term, such as planning for and going to a folk festival or a skiing holiday at some time in the future. All these techniques, whether short- or long-term, are geared to providing the individual with the pleasant feelings associated with good hedonic tone or, in other words, keeping themselves happy (Thayer 1989). These techniques, however, do not always work. If they did, the obvious logical conclusion is that people would be in pleasant states of mind, would be happy, all the time. This is clearly not the case. People seem to be somewhat ineffective in their mood management and to deal with this ineffectiveness by developing some tolerance for unpleasant mood states.

This analysis of the tactical manipulations of arousal to maintain short term hedonic tone in normal day to day living provides an essential contrast which makes it possible to define and understand addictions because addictive activities are chosen to replace and improve upon these normal coping strategies. In contrast to this normal state of poorly managed uncertainty and acquired tolerance for aversive states, the core of the addictive process can easily be seen as the discovery and continuous use by the individual of relatively reliable and effective methods which *do* enable him to manipulate arousal and hedonic tone in the directions he wants – reliably and immediately.

(Brown 1991b: 7)

It has already been pointed out that many of the various forms of arousal seeking behaviour engaged in by soccer hooligans can be recognized as attempts to generate the pleasant feelings associated with high arousal in the paratelic and negativistic states. Similarly to the important role that the management of felt arousal has in the development of other addictions, such as gambling and eating addictions (Brown 1991a, b; Kerr *et al.* 1994), arousal and the management of mood play a crucial role in the development of the superthugs' addiction to violence. In Brown's model there are seven fundamental stages in the development of an addiction (there are twelve stages in total, five of which are concerned with the period after addictive behaviour has become established). In Figure 7.1 these seven stages have been adapted to show how soccer hooligan behaviour develops into an addiction.

The subjective emotional experiences associated with soccer hooliganism mean that those who regularly perpetrate aggressive and violent hooligan acts are likely to be involved in a relatively narrow or specialized range of similar offences. It is also likely that the individuals involved are vulnerable, owing to, for example, limited access to rewarding experiences in other aspects of their daily lives. The powerful emotional reactions generated by aggressive and violent hooligan acts bring about mood changes associated with high arousal and are likely to be perceived as pleasant by the individual, thus providing him with improved quality of hedonic tone. As time goes on, the violent hooligan activity becomes increasingly more salient, with everyday life becoming increasingly dominated by fantasizing about and planning the next opportunity for violence. Consequently, the hooligan is emotionally rewarded by thinking about violence, preparing for it and then, following the action of 'steaming in', recollecting what took place. This would involve not only recollections of pleasant levels of felt arousal and felt negativism, but also felt transactional outcome and feelings of being strong, triumphant and proud. By increasing and repeated involvement in violent soccer thuggery, reinforced by positive feedback loops, further reductions in the alternative possibilities for rewarding experiences take place. Repeated participation in violent activities now takes place in cycles or episodes, which might obviously coincide with regularly occurring soccer games, and especially games involving teams with accompanying rival gangs and a history of violent activity in past confrontations. Over a series of games or perhaps a whole soccer season, these repeated episodes of hooligan fighting come together as a serial of aggressive and violent hooligan behaviour.

In time, more extreme risks are taken in order to achieve the same pleasant hedonic feelings, with enforced periods of non-hooligan activity

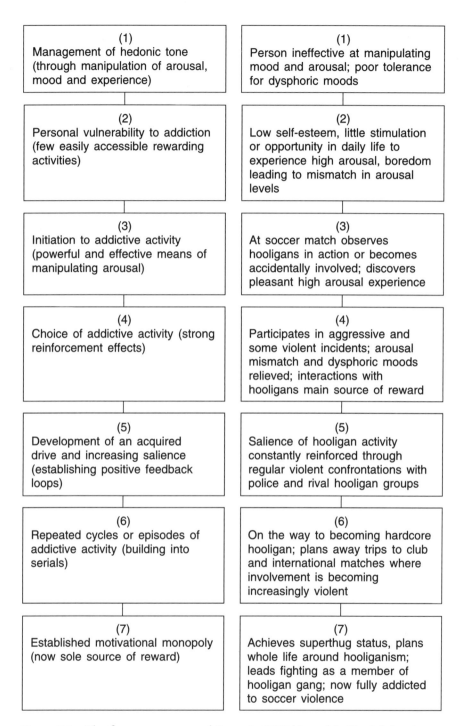

Figure 7.1 The first seven stages of Brown's (1991b) model. The left-hand panels contain the stages of development of addictive behaviour in general. The right-hand panels refer specifically to the development of addiction to soccer hooliganism.

leading to the feelings of restlessness and irritability often experienced in withdrawal. The hooligan offender is now caught up in an escalating cycle of confrontation and violence in which the soccer hooligan activity is probably the only option available for effectively managing hedonic tone. Consequently, for the soccer thug soccer hooliganism may become his only source of pleasure and reward, often to the detriment of most other aspects of daily life.

At times, perhaps between soccer matches or seasons, hooligans may experience low self-esteem accompanied by feelings of being out of control and a general inability successfully to 'kick the habit'. However, the World Cup and European Championship tournaments, which take place outside the domestic soccer season, may provide the superthugs (should England be participating) with additional opportunities for hooligan violence in a period in which they might otherwise be experiencing unpleasant dysphoria and generally poor hedonic tone.

Like those who attempt to kick other addictive behaviour, for those who attempt to give up hooligan violence there is always a danger of reverting. This reversion may occur quite rapidly, even after long periods of abstinence, to the frequency and intensity of previous activity. Stimulated by more extreme relapse-provoking stimuli, such as television or media reports or perhaps contact with former hooligan 'mates', once again the individual relapses into a pattern of recurring violence (that is, unless the former hooligan has been able to bring about a substantial change in the manner of his management of hedonic tone). This is a subject that is addressed in the following chapter, where the additional stages of Brown's model, concerning the recovery and rehabilitation of former addicts, will be related to soccer superthugs. Before this there is one final aspect of the psychological characteristics of soccer superthugs that should be considered.

Are soccer superthugs real psychopaths?

It has been suggested by some writers that the hooligan leaders are 'psychologically-disturbed' (Taylor 1982: 170) or 'disturbed and psychopathic' (Robins 1984: 16). Graef (1993: 21) stated: 'Of course, the ringleaders, the hard core, should be identified and punished – the police are doing their best to achieve that. Indeed some are psychopaths who need treatment. But the huge number of others being swept along into violence need other outlets for their energy.' Is this view of soccer superthugs correct? Are they subject to some kind of personality disorder and are they really psychopathic?

In recent years the DSM-III-R Classification System (1987), developed in the United States, has proved useful for psychiatrists and psychologists when they are classifying mental disorders. The DSM-III-R criteria for 'antisocial personality disorder', the American term for psychopathic behaviour, requires that two important features of an individual's behaviour be taken into account. First, even though the diagnosis cannot be applied to anyone under eighteen, the behaviour has to be longstanding, with substantial evidence of antisocial behaviour before the age of fifteen. Included in such evidence would be behaviour such as habitual lying, early aggressive and sexual behaviour, excessive drinking, theft, vandalism and chronic rule violation at home and at school. In addition, according to the DSM-III-R criteria the individual's present antisocial behaviour must be manifested in at least four of the following: shows inconsistent work or school behaviour; repeatedly performs antisocial behaviour that is liable to result in arrest; is irritable and aggressive leading to repeated fights or assaults; repeatedly fails to honour financial commitments; is impulsive or fails to plan ahead; lies repeatedly; engages in reckless behaviour without regard to the personal safety of his or her self or others; is irresponsible with regard to parental duty; engages in sexual promiscuity; shows a lack of remorse upon harming others.

If the DSM-III-R criteria are examined carefully, four criteria from the list above might be applied to the soccer superthugs. They do repeatedly perform antisocial behaviour that is liable to result in arrest and they are often involved in repeated fights or assaults, but are not necessarily generally irritable and aggressive. The soccer hooligan superthugs do engage in reckless behaviour without regard to the personal safety of themselves or others and they often revel in the injuries they have inflicted on rival hooligans, rather than feeling remorse. Although superthugs' characteristic behaviour would appear to fulfil four of the criteria for antisocial personality disorder, little is known, by this author at least, about their circumstances and behaviour before the age of fifteen. While the DSM-III-R concentrates on indicators of antisocial behaviour other approaches have focused on personality factors using psychometric measures (Hare 1986).

In the United Kingdom the Mental Health Act of 1983, which considered psychopathic disorder as a form of mental illness, defined psychopathic disorder as 'a persistent disorder of the mind which results in abnormally aggressive or seriously irresponsible conduct on the part of the patient' (see Gregory 1987). This definition is somewhat more subjective than American ones and specific diagnostic checklist criteria have not yet been developed in Britain (Farrington 1991).

According to Farrington (1991), current research is concentrated on the extent to which psychopathy should be regarded as a unitary construct. He drew attention to work which showed that Hare's Psychopathy Checklist scores could be indicative of both personality traits such as low emotionality, guilt, remorse and empathy and an antisocial lifestyle (Harpur *et al.* 1988, 1989). Reference is also made to Blackburn's (1987) research work, which has separated psychopaths into 'primary' or non-anxious psychopaths and 'secondary' psychopaths who do exhibit anxiety. These results have led Blackburn (1987) to the conclusion that antisocial lifestyles may or may not be linked to an antisocial personality.

The reversal theory view of psychopathy

The trait-based approaches described above conceptualize psychopaths as being psychopathic most of the time. The reversal theory perspective is different, incorporating both dominance and state explanations of this type of behaviour. With respect to the dominance characteristics of psychopaths, Apter (1982) claimed that their behaviour has three important characteristics that differentiate them from non-psychopathic individuals. Psychopaths were thought to be paratelic dominant, to use extreme measures to obtain satisfying levels of arousal and to exhibit a tendency to attempt to gain excitement through negativism. At face value, all three of these features would appear to be present in the behaviour of at least some hardcore hooligans.

Later empirical work by Thomas-Peter (1988; Thomas-Peter and McDonagh 1988) questioned the link between psychopathic behaviour and paratelic dominance. As described in Chapter 3, empirical work (e.g. Jones 1981; Bowers 1985) had shown clear links between delinquency and paratelic dominance. However, in a study (Thomas-Peter and McDonagh 1988) that compared the telic dominance scores of an undifferentiated group of psychopaths with the scores of a normal control group, psychopaths were found to be more telic dominant than the control group, thus contradicting the paratelic dominance hypothesis. In addition, Thomas-Peter and McDonagh (1988), using a similar methodology to Blackburn (1979), divided the psychopaths into the same four groups. Following further analysis, incorporating primary and secondary groups and a group that combined controlled and inhibited groups, it was shown that neither primary nor secondary psychopaths were more paratelic dominant than the combined group.

Apter (1988) argued that the real clue to understanding psychopathic behaviour might lie in the link between negativism dominance and psychopathy. Further empirical work by Thomas-Peter (1993) did produce findings that supported the view that primary and secondary psychopaths would display higher negativism scores than control group subjects and other offenders. Both groups scored higher than control subjects. More specifically, the primary psychopathic group scored significantly higher on overall negativism dominance scores and on proactive negativism subscale scores than the secondary group, thus suggesting a clear link between negativism and psychopathy.

Thomas-Peter (1992) suggested that further investigation of possible differences in the motivation behind offending in primary and secondary psychopaths was needed. He hypothesized that primary psychopathic offending arises from 'neurotic conflict' and secondary psychopathic offending from 'more hedonistic psychological demands'. Using McDermott's (1988a & b) reversal theory distinction between reactive and proactive negativism, Thomas-Peter (1992) went on to hypothesize that secondary psychopaths are more likely to offend reactively whereas primary psychopaths will be more likely 'to commission acts of aggression as a deliberate and purposeful means of self-enhancement or excitement seeking'. Thus, if Thomas-Peter's (1992) hypothesis is correct, we might assume that superthugs, if they are psychopaths, fall into the category of primary psychopaths.

As a result of the real psychopath being locked or stuck in a particular state combination, his or her behaviour remains relatively constant. Unlike other people, psychopaths are state 'inhibited' and therefore insensitive to stimuli that, in other people, would ordinarily induce reversals. The psychopathic soccer hooligan is likely to be stuck in a metamotivational state combination of paratelic-negativistic-autic-mastery.

While some superthugs show all the signs of being clinical psychopaths, other hardcore hooligans are not. Their psychopathic behaviour only occurs on match days and their behaviour remains relatively 'normal' through the rest of the week. The aggressive and violent behaviour of these hooligans has a temporary quality. The reversal mechanisms of these 'temporary psychopaths' are flexible and uninhibited, allowing them to reverse into the necessary conjunction of states on match days, without which psychopathic-type behaviour would not take place. Consequently most soccer hooligans, even of the superthug type, are not psychopaths in the traditional clinical sense, but it is likely that a few can be classified as clinical psychopaths.

It is only through the metamotivational level approach of reversal theory that state-based explanations of hooligan and delinquent behaviour are possible. Other theories have largely failed to account for soccer hooligan violence that has a temporary or part-time nature.

Closing comments

Through Brown's (1991a,b) Hedonic Tone Management Model of Addictions and reversal theory, on which the model is based, an understanding of the strong psychological processes underlying hardcore or superthug hooligan behaviour has been elicited. The reader should now be in a good position to answer the question asked repeatedly by those who are involved with the soccer hooliganism problem and posed earlier in this chapter. 'Why is it that individuals (sometimes educated, financially well-off and from a "good background") engage in hooligan activity, when, on the surface at least, there would appear to be no real need to do so?' In the final chapter, our reversal theory foundation will be used to discuss and answer all the crucial questions about soccer hooliganism asked at the end of Chapter 1.

References

Apter, M. J. (1982). *The Experience of Motivation*. London: Academic Press.
Apter, M. J. (1988). *Reversal Theory: Motivation, Emotion and Personality*. London: Routledge.

Blackburn, R. (1979). 'Psychopathy and personality: the dimensionality of self-report and behaviour rating data in abnormal offenders'. *British Journal of Clinical and Social Psychology*, 18, 111–19.

Blackburn, R. (1987). 'Two scales for the assessment of personality deviation in antisocial populations'. *Personality and Individual Differences*, 8, 81–93.

Bowers, A. J. (1985). 'Reversals, delinquency and disruption'. *British Journal of Clinical Psychology*, 25, 303–4.

Brown, R. I. F. (1988). 'Reversal theory and subjective experience in the explanation of addiction and relapse', in M. J. Apter, J. H. Kerr and M. P. Cowles (eds) *Progress in Reversal Theory*. Amsterdam: North-Holland Elsevier, pp. 191–211.

Brown, R. I. F. (1991a). 'Gaming, gambling and other addictive play', in J. H. Kerr and M. J. Apter (eds) *Adult Play*. Amsterdam: Swets and Zeitlinger, pp. 101–18.

Brown, R. I. F. (1991b). 'Mood management, self states as goals and addiction models of criminal behaviour'. Paper presented at the British Psychological Society Division of Criminal and Legal Psychology and Department of Psychology, Rampton Hospital Conference, Addicted to Crime, Nottingham.

Buford, B. (1991). *Among the Thugs*. London: Secker & Warburg.

Canter, D., Comber, M. and Uzzell, D. L. (1989). *Football in its place*. Routledge: London, New York.

Corrigan, P. (1977). *Schooling the Smash Street Kids*. London: Macmillan.

Darbyshire, N. (1987). 'Operation Own Goal'. *The Independent*, 9 May.

Dunning, E., Maguire, J. A., Murphy, P. J. and Williams, J. M. (1982). 'The social roots of football hooliganism'. *Leisure Studies*, 2, 139–56.

Farrington, D. F. (1991). 'Antisocial personality from childhood to adulthood'. *The Psychologist: Bulletin of the British Psychological Society*, 4, 389–94.

Graef, R. (1993). 'The way to handle him'. *Daily Telegraph*, 15 October, 21.

Gregory, R. L. (1987). *The Oxford Companion to the Mind*. Oxford: Oxford University Press.

Hardy, A. (1985). 'Five years for hooligan "general"'. *Guardian*, 22 May.

Hare, R. D. (1986). 'Twenty years of experience with the Checkley psychopath', in W. H. Reid, D. Dorr, J. I. Walker and J. W. Bonner (eds) *Unmasking the Psychopath: Antisocial Personality and Related Syndromes*. New York: Norton, pp. 3–27.

Harpur, T. J., Hakistan, A. R. and Hare, R. D. (1988). 'Factor structure of the Psychopathy Checklist'. *Journal of Consulting and Clinical Psychology*, 56, 741–7.

Harpur, T. J., Hare, R. D. and Hakistan, A. R. (1989). 'Two-factor conceptualization of psychopathy: construct validity and assessment implications'. *Psychological Assessment: a Journal of Consulting and Clinical Psychology*, 1, 6–17.

Johnson, A. (1988). 'Police covert operation sends "Para Army" hooligans to gaol'. *Guardian*, 2 June.

Jones, R. (1981). 'Reversals, delinquency and fun'. *European Journal of Humanistic Psychology*, 9, 237–40.

Keating, F. (1985). 'Fan who get their kicks off the field'. *Guardian*, 16 August.

Keel, P. (1987a). 'Terraces of terror'. *Guardian*, 9 May.

Keel, P. (1987b). 'Slashed fan identified mob boss, court told'. *Guardian*, 8 January.

Keel, P. (1987c). 'Diary of a soccer thug'. *Guardian*, 9 May.

Kerr, J. H., Brown, R. I. F. and Frank-Ragan, E. (1994). 'Taking risks with health'. *Patient Education and Counselling*, in the press.

Mc Dermott, M. R. (1988a). 'Measuring Rebelliousness: The Development of the

Negativism Dominance Scale', in M. J. Apter, J. H. Kerr and M. P. Cowles (eds) *Progress in Reversal Theory*. Amsterdam: North-Holland Elsevier, pp. 297–312.

Mc Dermott, M. R. (1988b). 'Recognising rebelliousness: The ecological validity of the negativism dominance scale', in M. J. Apter, J. H. Kerr and M. P. Cowles (eds) *Progress in Reversal Theory*. Amsterdam: North-Holland Elsevier, pp. 297–312.

Marsh, P. (1978). *Aggro: the Illusion of Violence*. London: Dent.

Mills, H. (1987). 'Diary gave details of thugs' trail of terror'. *The Independent*, 9 May.

Popplewell, O. (1986). *Committee of Inquiry into Crowd Safety and Control at Sports Grounds: Final Report*. Chairman. Mr Justice Popplewell. London: HMSO.

Robins, D. (1984). *We Hate Humans*. Harmondsworth: Penguin.

Sharratt, T. (1989). 'Police team targets hooligan "generals"'. *Guardian*, 13 September.

Taylor, E. (1984). 'I was a soccer hooligan – Class of 64'. *Guardian*, 28 March.

Taylor, I. (1976). 'Spectator violence around football: the rise and fall of the 'Working Class Weekend'. *Research Papers in Physical Education*, 4(1) 4–9.

Taylor, I. (1982). 'On the sports violence question: soccer hooliganism revisited', in J. Hargreaves (ed.) *Sport, Culture and Society*. London: Routledge and Kegan Paul.

Tendler, S. (1987). 'The hunting of the Headhunters'. *The Times*, 9 May.

Thayer, R. E. (1989). *The Biopsychology of Mood and Arousal*. New York: Oxford University Press.

Thomas-Peter, B. A. (1988). 'Psychopathy and telic dominance', in M. J. Apter, J. H. Kerr & M. P. Cowles (eds) *Progress in Reversal Theory*. Amsterdam: North-Holland, pp. 235–44.

Thomas-Peter, B. A. (1992). 'The classification of psychopathy: a review of the Hare vs Blackburn debate'. *Personality and Individual Differences*, 13(3) 337–42.

Thomas-Peter, B. A. (1993). 'Negativism and the classification of psychopathy', in J. H. Kerr, S. Murgatroyd and M. J. Apter (eds) *Advances in Reversal Theory*. Amsterdam: Swets and Zeitlinger, pp. 313–24.

Thomas-Peter, B. A. and McDonagh, J. D. (1988). 'Motivational dominance in psychopaths'. *British Journal of Clinical Psychology*, 27, 153–8.

Ward, C. (1989). *Steaming In*. London: Simon and Schuster.

Williams, J., Dunning, E. and Murphy, P. (1984). *Hooligans Abroad*. London: Routledge and Kegan Paul.

PROSPECTUS FOR AN IMPROVED UNDERSTANDING OF SOCCER HOOLIGANISM

In an attempt to establish just what kind of problem soccer hooliganism presents, a number of fundamental questions were proposed at the end of Chapter 1. Providing satisfactory answers to those questions is the key to gaining a real understanding of the motivation behind soccer hooliganism. Each of these questions will now be directly addressed in this final chapter.

Are soccer hooligans really moronic idiots or drunken yobs, as they are so often portrayed in the media?

One common view of soccer hooligan and delinquent behaviour is that it is a mindless activity, engaged in by yobs or morons who are often drunk. Arguments presented earlier in this book have underlined the fact that most, if not all, soccer hooligan behaviour is non-serious and has no particular function beyond immediate sensation and the fun and enjoyment that it can provide (i.e. paratelic-oriented). If hooliganism does have a purpose then it is merely to maximize the immediate sensation and rich emotional rewards that accompany taking risks and being negativistic (Jones 1981; Reade 1984; Bowers 1988; Kerr 1988; Apter 1992).

It is thought that alcohol has a biphasic effect (Thayer 1989). Initially, by suppressing the inhibitory synapses in the brain earlier than the excitatory synapses, positive moods are increased and negative moods decreased (see Hull and Bond 1986). As tension and inhibitions are released, the person feels stimulated, excited and more self-confident. After a short time, alcohol can have a depressant effect, as the brain's excitatory synapses also become suppressed and the stimulating effects are cancelled out. The person's sensory and motor functions may become slowed, accompanied by feelings of drowsiness. When soccer hooligans drink they do so to boost felt arousal and enhance pleasant moods, thus adding to the effects of other sources of increased arousal at soccer games and further contributing to their overall feelings of elation. Some hooligans, however, namely the topmen and superthugs (Chapter 7), are reported not to drink alcohol before engaging in violence. This allows them to keep their senses fully atuned during the fighting.

In general, the people involved in soccer hooliganism are not morons and are sometimes quite intelligent and creative. Consequently, to describe soccer hooliganism as mindless behaviour by drunken morons is completely to misunderstand the motivational processes involved.

Is soccer hooliganism a direct result of unemployment and material deprivation?

'Popular wisdom' suggests that delinquents and soccer hooligans are unemployed and originate from deprived working class backgrounds. This view may have arisen partially as a result of sociological explanations that have linked the emergence of soccer hooliganism to aspects of working class culture (see Chapter 1). For example, Dunning and his colleagues (1982) argued that soccer hooliganism was an expression of the violent masculine style associated with rough lower working class tradition and claimed that the development of the violent style among males of poorer communities was a direct outcome of 'the multiple deprivations from which such communities suffer' (Williams *et al.* 1984: 13).

In addition, Taylor (1971) talked about the unemployed, the unemployable and the lower-paid working class as being important in the development of soccer hooliganism in the 1960s. However, later (Taylor 1976: 4) he conceded that 'the frustrations of working-class youth at employment or in education are in fact minimal'. Taylor's (1976) hypothesis now was that commercial alternatives for youth leisure at the weekend and during the week had multiplied and that, as a result, the overall significance of the 'working class weekend' had become considerably diminished. This, he argued, provoked working class youth to defend their traditional weekend culture by resorting to soccer hooligan tactics. Later still, Taylor (1987: 179) stated that 'the violence in Brussels (and indeed the violence of soccer supporters of England in the World Cup in Spain) could not have been committed by the most economically deprived, or objectively lumpen-proletarian, English workers.' Dunning *et al.* (1986) also conceded that not all hooligans were from the working class.

Although the 'working class' theories have been extended and developed over the years, at times the theoretical arguments appear to be somewhat contradictory. For instance, it would seem that while on the one hand it was argued that soccer hooligan violence emerged from the deprivation of the lower strata of the working class communities, on the other it was thought to be a result of too much variety in leisure opportunities for working class youth. It appears that either early explanations were incomplete and missed aspects of soccer hooliganism that were later addressed, or the socioeconomic character of soccer spectators and/or hooligans has changed over time. In a letter to the *Observer* newspaper, Davies (1985) claimed that regular football watchers were well aware of the fact that soccer-related violence in the mid 1980s was different from that of the 1970's and could not be tied into unemployment and deprivation. He wrote,

> ... it is ridiculous to claim that football violence is the result of un-employment and urban deprivation, as though 'they can't help it, poor dears'. Any genuine football fan will tell you that the current plague of violence is led by affluent young gangsters, relieving the tensions built up by their newly fashionable white-collar jobs. Those responsible will tell you themselves – with great pride.

Figures from Harrington (1968) and Trivizas (1980) show that the vast majority of those charged with offences related to soccer were employed, albeit largely in the unskilled or semi-skilled occupational groups. As far as soccer spectators in general are concerned, in 1983 the largest proportions were found to be from the professional, employer or managerial group and the skilled manual group (General Household Survey 1983, cited in Canter *et al.* 1989). These figures are concerned with fans and not necessarily hooligans, but the trials of top hooligans and superthugs described in Chapter 7 showed that the majority were not unemployed and some, at least, had 'professional' jobs (Keel 1987). Other soccer hooligans had been public school (Buford 1991) or university students (Taylor 1984).

From the reversal theory point of view, to present arguments for either lower class material inadequacies or, conversely, affluence as being the root cause of the soccer hooligan violence is to miss a much more crucial point. Reade's (1984) statement about delinquency and vandalism adds to the present discussion. His comments apply equally well to soccer hooliganism:

> If it could be shown that those who commit acts of vandalism are those who lack the material or cultural provisions mentioned above, the problem would be well on the way towards being solved ... On the one hand, we know that young people who have been brought up at quite low material and educational standards, whether in absolute terms or relative to other groups, in society, often commit no vandalism. On the other hand, we know that quite privileged young people often do commit such acts. And in the case of unemployment, at the moment the form of deprivation causing greatest concern, there is again little evidence of any causal connection.
>
> (Reade 1984: 135)

If the term 'deprivation' should appear in the context of a reversal theory discussion of soccer hooliganism, then it should be deprivation in the sense of a lack of opportunity to experience a full range of satisfying and rewarding experiences. A kind of 'psychological deprivation' or 'metamotivational deprivation', as it might be labelled, can occur even in cases of prosperity and affluence (Klapp 1986; see also Chapter 3). Reversal theorists argue that 'good' mental health is maintained through spending time in all possible combinations of the different metamotivational states (Murgatroyd and Apter 1986). For some, such as addicted soccer hooligans, who become 'trapped' or 'stuck' in one particular metamotivational State combination, the opportunity to enjoy satisfying and rewarding experiences is limited to hooligan violence, which becomes their sole source of satisfaction (Brown 1988, 1991a, b).

Even for the much maligned members of the lower working class, the list of diverse activities that are worth doing and could provide a self-fulfilling experience is almost endless. The process of finding, choosing and maintaining an interest in any activity starts in childhood and continues into adulthood. Apter (1992: 193), echoing the words of others, struck the right note when he said,

> Specifically, what is needed is for youngsters not just to be taught, but to be taught how to teach themselves. What should be imparted is the open-ended skill of learning new skills, together with a fascination for the world around in all its aspects, an enthusiasm for new challenges and a belief in the possibility of self-improvement.

This will not occur if the person's learning experience is restricted or distorted in some way. For example, Van der Molen (1985, 1986) has pointed out that, with regard to the telic and paratelic metamotivational states, the development of what he has called a 'negative learning spiral' may restrict or prevent open-ended learning. Negative learning spirals are thought to begin when the natural movement between telic and paratelic (arousal avoiding and arousal seeking) states breaks down, preventing concomitant learning experiences. If a person is somehow 'deprived' of experience in the paratelic state, or the opportunity satisfactorily to assimilate paratelic experience while in the telic state, the person will not develop a broad enough repertoire of skills and knowledge. The person in the telic state then becomes dependent on a few restricted and similar strategies for dealing with problems. This may lead to a loss of confidence and make satisfying experiences in the paratelic state even harder to achieve. In this way, a negative learning spiral is built up (Apter and Kerr 1991), and in a similar way, irrespective of socioeconomic background, being deprived of rewarding, self-fulfilling experiences can lead to involvement in soccer hooligan violence. Conversely, 'positive learning spirals' are characterized by frequent movement between telic and paratelic states, allowing the person to develop adequate skills, knowledge and the confidence to deal with life's difficulties.

What motivates people to take unnecessary risks, in terms of physical injury or imprisonment, by fighting with rival hooligans or confronting the police?

For the reader who has followed the arguments developed through the earlier chapters of this book, the answer to this question should already be clear. The first point to make is that there is a play-fight element in much hooligan fighting which contributes to what Marsh (1978) has called 'the illusion of violence'. In other words, soccer-related aggro and violence generally appears to be much worse than it actually is. 'Serious injuries on the football terraces have been as rare as those on the South Coast beaches or the cinemas and dance halls of the 1950s. Things like malicious woundings occur elsewhere and their frequency increases in step with the loss of opportunity for social fighting' (Marsh 1978: 143; see also Ward 1989: 7). While a number of stabbings and vicious slashings with 'Stanley' knives, along with other types of serious assault, have also sometimes occurred, the most common form of fighting has been with fists and boots. Over a thirty-year period, in which hooligan fighting has involved hundreds, if not thousands, of people, deaths and serious injury that have occurred as a direct outcome of hooligan violence have been relatively few. The deaths that occurred at the Heysel Stadium disaster were the result of a hooligan charge, but they came about as a result of the collapse of a retaining wall, rather than as a direct result of people being beaten up or stabbed.

In the enjoyment of soccer hooligan violence, injuries and occasional deaths are necessary ingredients. According to reversal theory, soccer hooliganism takes place within a protective frame in which the hooligan feels relatively safe, but in which high levels of felt arousal can be experienced to the full. 'That danger produces arousal hardly needs to be pointed out, but if such arousal can be experienced within a protective frame we have a potent way of creating enormous excitement' (Apter, 1991: 20). Without the element of danger, excitement would be much reduced or even absent and the hooligan game would be spoilt. Similarly, without a risk factor many activities, such as parachuting, mountaineering, motor racing, circus daredevil acts, aerobatic air shows and fire-eating, would be much less stimulating and exciting for participants and spectators alike.

Taking part in soccer hooliganism does involve a degree of unnecessary risk-taking and is therefore an example of paradoxical behaviour. It is behaviour that is certainly not necessary for biological survival and may well be injurious to the participant's physical health. However, though it may seem difficult to understand, participation in hooliganism *can* contribute to the individual's *mental* health. For those people who spend long periods of time in particular metamotivational states where, for instance, the opportunities for experiencing high felt arousal or positive hedonic tone are limited, hooliganism provides them with a chance to redress the balance. This is especially true for paratelic dominant, arousal seeking individuals who, in need of stimulation, engage in antisocial behaviour like soccer hooliganism because it involves risk, novelty and variation.

The build-up of unpleasant mismatches in arousal levels, perhaps at work where the most common operative states may be telic-conformity, can, for example, be offset by soccer hooligan behaviour, governed as it is by the metamotivational state combination of paratelic-negativism. What is more, the pleasant hedonic tone arising from high levels of felt arousal and felt negativism, associated with some delinquent and hooligan acts, is very likely to be reinforcing and to cause the hooligan to repeat the behaviour on future occasions. This is equally true of the metamotivational state combination of autic-mastery, which also has a strong role to play in the soccer hooligan experience. Here hooligan activities help the individual to cope with non-preferred levels of felt transactional outcome and poor self tone experienced in daily living. Thus, in fulfilling the necessary reversal theory requisite for maintaining 'good' mental health (that is, frequent movement between and experience in all metamotivational states), the metamotivational combination of paratelic-negativistic-autic-mastery, achieved through hooligan activity, takes on added importance.

Why do people suddenly become aggressive and violent towards others who have done them no harm?

As outlined in Chapter 5, aggression and anger are closely linked to arousal and arise as the result of particular combinations of metamotivational states. Within these particular combinations, the telic and paratelic states play an important role. The metamotivational state combination operative during most types of soccer hooligan activity is paratelic-negativistic-autic-mastery. The paratelic-negativism element within this combination (with accompanying high levels of felt arousal and felt negativism) gives rise to the type of provocative, playful paratelic aggression that characterizes so many examples of soccer hooligan activity. Hooligan behaviour in these circumstances is not necessarily malicious, but is engaged in with the major purpose of generating excitement and the pleasures of release from rules.

Hooligan behaviour is likely to become especially malicious and violent towards others when the paratelic state reverses to telic, producing a new state combination of telic-negativistic-autic-mastery. The resulting emotion of anger is an unpleasant high arousal emotion, often directed against other people, which can result in serious physical assault.

The hardmen and superthugs of soccer hooligan violence were discussed in Chapter 7. This special type of soccer hooligan engages in extreme hooligan acts and is addicted to hooligan violence. When a 'ruck' occurs he is usually to be found in the thick of the fighting. These soccer hooligans are totally reliant on fighting to bridge what for them, in their daily lives, is a huge 'gap' in hedonic tone (Brown 1991b). Although some delinquent and hooligan behaviour may be misleadingly labelled as psychopathic, some soccer hooligans (those involved in the most malicious, violent and aggressive behaviour) may well be psychopaths. If this is the case, it is unlikely that these individuals will be satisfied only with violent confrontations in and around soccer.

Hippo explained: 'Us lot, the blokes who really go to fight, we don't just fight inside the football ground. We fight outside the ground. We go to discos and fight. We go to nightclubs and have a fight. In a pub we have a fight. Wherever we go we fight . . . No, we don't do it for money. Hell's Angels, mercenary groups, the villains round 'ere, they will do it for the money. But you've got others, they just go around and they just wanna do it for the *feeling* of smashing someone's head open. I mean – sometimes I just feel I wanna get hold of some cunt and lay him over a railing and splatter him. Other times you may feel sorry after. But not often. (*Laughs*.) Mostly you just wanna hit someone every time.'

(Robins 1984: 107–8)

Why are the measures taken by the authorities apparently so ineffective in dealing with soccer hooligans?

Another aspect of 'popular wisdom' about soccer hooliganism is that the government and judiciary should 'get tough' with soccer hooligans. In other words, the government should pass new laws so that hooligans would receive larger fines and longer prison sentences. In 1990, for example, 600 arrests were made following outbreaks of soccer hooligan violence in a number of *English towns* after England's defeat by West Germany *in Italy* during the 1990 World Cup. In parliament, the British Deputy Prime Minister, Geoffrey Howe, called on the courts to hand down effective sentences for convicted soccer hooligans. One newspaper headline, 'Howe says hit hooligans hard', reflected the mood of the authorities. Indeed, many of the punishments previously handed out to soccer hooligans have been harsh and even unjust in comparison to the punishment for other more serious crimes. In contrast to these calls for more stringent measures, Bowers (1988: 234) stated:

> We have recently seen the popular press and public figures extolling the virtues of exemplary prison sentences as deterrents of delinquent acts; the current preoccupation with 'soccer hooliganism' in particular has led to the assumption that the threat of seriously aversive consequences will moderate the violent and aggressive behaviours which are associated with many young football enthusiasts. However, behind the idea of a deterrent lies the assumption that the acts that it is designed to suppress are committed in a calculated, premeditated and goal-oriented manner. The present study suggests that this is less likely to be the case for adolescent delinquents, the very group for whom deterrent punishments are advocated, than for their non-delinquent peers.

Take, for example, the so-called 'short sharp shock' detention centre treatment for delinquent and hooligan offenders, implemented by the

Thatcher Government. Jones (1981) has contended that these programmes are largely ineffective because staff were unaware that, first, many hooligans and delinquents are paratelic-oriented and, second, hooligan and delinquent activities are mostly carried out when those concerned are in the paratelic state (Jones 1981). Consequently, when staff confronted offenders with the seriousness of their offences they received a poor response. The paratelic-oriented offenders considered their delinquent activities to have been immense fun and did not consider that they needed treatment at all. Walter (1978: 2), a colleague of Jones, wrote:

> Boys are more concerned with getting out of trouble than with analysing how they got into trouble. For them, trouble means getting caught and being sent to an approved school. Their concern is to get out of approved school. Trouble as defined by (the approved school) staff and other agencies, namely offences committed and anti-social behaviour, is not something boys see as requiring explanation.

Owing to their predominantly paratelic-negativistic metamotivational pattern, offenders are likely to experience delinquency treatment programmes as thoroughly boring. One offender on the programme was reported as saying 'in supervision you sit down in a boring old chair and talk about how we're getting on and things' (Jones 198: 239). Individuals who much prefer high arousal and excitement are forced to spend long periods in a state of low arousal in detention. Once again, this leads to mismatches in levels of preferred and actual felt arousal and contributes to a build-up of tension and stress, the very problem that led to the hooligan and delinquent activities in the first place. Such attempts at treatment would appear to be largely counter productive.

There are of course some metamotivational conditions under which the counselling approach described above might work. If the offender has the paratelic and negavistic metamotivational states operative then little response can be expected. However, if a reversal has taken place to the telic-conformist metamotivational state combination then this approach will be more likely to initiate a more serious (and for the staff more appropriate) response from the offender. It is only when offenders are in the telic and conformist metamotivational states that they will be able to view their behaviour from a more critical and long-term perspective. In addition, if the offenders are also in the sympathy and alloic states (where the concern is with others) this will assist in the counselling process. For example, it is only when the offender is in the alloic and sympathy states that feelings of guilt might be experienced. Shared group experiences may prove effective in inducing and maintaining these two metamotivational states (Apter 1989).

Alternatively, if intervention strategies that took more account of the paratelic orientation of many soccer hooligans were used to show offenders how they might achieve fun, excitement and high arousal from activities other than soccer hooligan or delinquent activities, they might be more successful. This theme is addressed in the next section of this chapter.

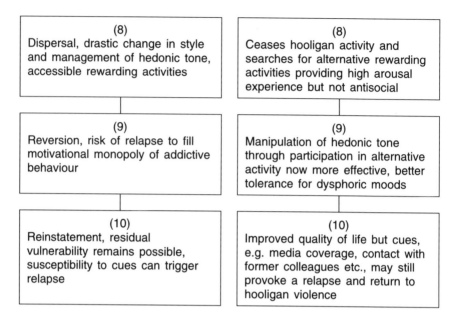

Figure 8.1 The three stages of Brown's (1991b) model concerned with intervention and addictions. The left-hand panels refer to addictions in general and the right-hand panels to soccer hooliganism in particular.

What will work? Possibilities for intervention with hooligans

In Chapter 7 the first seven stages of Brown's Hedonic Tone Management Model of Addictions were described and applied to soccer hooliganism. Brown's model is actually a twelve-stage model and three of the last five stages concentrate on intervention and are therefore appropriate for inclusion here (see Figure 8.1). By stage 7 in the addiction model, soccer hooligan activities have become an established motivational monopoly, providing the sole source of reward for the addicted hooligan. In other words, violent hooligan behaviour has become the most salient feature of the hardcore hooligan's life. The individual is now preoccupied with, and craves, hooligan violence and this increasingly brings about a deterioration of social behaviour in a number of well-recognized ways, common to most other addictions. These include: increased conflict with, for example, friends and relatives (thus further increases the salience of the behaviour); an inability to restrict hooligan activity, leading to a degree of loss of control; a reaction effect at the cessation of hooligan violence, causing an even greater desire for relief (thus also increasing salience and the need to repeat the behaviour as soon as possible); increasing tolerance, so that increased amounts of hooligan activity are needed to produce the same emotional effects; withdrawal effects when hooliganism ceases, causing unpleasant feelings and finally a tendency to relapse and repeat the addictive behaviour (Brown 1991b).

One of the problems with suggesting strategies for intervention is that, over time, violent hooligan behaviour has become so entrenched, so reinforced, so caught up with eliminating dysphoric moods and attaining good hedonic tone, that it becomes difficult to extinguish. Steps 8, 9 and 10 of Brown's model describe how interventions to alleviate the problems of the addicted person might be approached. In step 8, the dispersal stage, it is necessary to bring about a drastic change in what Brown (1991b: 13) has termed 'the policy and style of management of hedonic tone'. The hooligan needs to be made aware of how the addictive process works, and, more specifically, the role of reinforcement and the positive feedback loops associated with hooligan activity needs to be understood. In addition, the hooligan needs to be confronted with the fact that ceasing involvement will, just as with other addictions, result in a period of distress characterized by unpleasant feelings and general dysphoria. As Brown (1991b: 20) pointed out,

> The major work of the period of dispersal lies in the revival of as many of the varied sources of reward in different areas of the subject's life as possible and the establishment of new ones. If the previous repertoire of easily accessible rewarding activities is to be revived and regenerated, careful consideration and planning with a high quality of decision making must be extended to every area of the person's life, working, domestic, social and recreational, etc. Better planning for the medium and long term manipulation of hedonic tone will make the short term, day to day, minute to minute, management of hedonic tone easier and restore the stable state of reward diversity (as opposed to specialism) or motivational pluralism.

The key factor in intervention treatment, based on this model, is to replace hooligan behaviour with some alternative form of rewarding activity or activities, which can provide the same levels of excitement and pleasure and intensity of experience but which are not antisocial. If this cannot be achieved, it is very likely that the hooligan will revert to hooligan fighting. It may take the ex-hooligan a considerable time, a matter of some years rather than days or months, to build up an effective change in the policy and style of hedonic tone management.

In the case of addiction to soccer hooligan violence there would seem to be three possible strategies (see Figure 8.2). First, hooligan fighting might be relocated to a context that is not antisocial, such as that associated with combat sports: boxing, judo or the Eastern martial arts. This strategy, however, would require the ex-hooligan to move away from negativistic activity, as most of these sports require a high degree of conformity to rules or etiquette. Second, activities that the hooligan engaged in before starting on a hooligan career might be regenerated. However, keep in mind

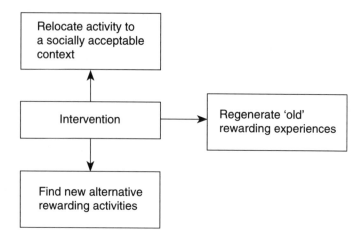

Figure 8.2 The three possible strategies for intervention treatment for soccer hooligans.

that these activities were rejected before as inadequate in producing the desired levels of hedonic tone, and so may not prove as effective as the third strategy. The third possibility is to find a new set of self-satisfying experiences. This approach offers perhaps the best option for successful treatment, as it would have added appeal, in terms of novelty, for producing paratelic-oriented experience. At the metamotivational level what is required here is a change from the well-entrenched state combinations of paratelic-negativism and autic-mastery associated with soccer hooligan acts to a state combination of paratelic-conformity and alloic-mastery or, in some circumstances, such as individual risk sports, perhaps autic-mastery.

There are examples of these different intervention strategies that have been found to work effectively with some other addictive behaviours. For example, thinking back to the activities of joyriders described in Chapter 3, one of the most successful ways of dealing with the problem has been to set up garages and race tracks where former joyriders can service their own vehicles and race against each other in a relatively safe environment (Thompson 1988). This strategy has the dual benefit of still allowing the joyriders to achieve the high arousal emotional states they desire and, at the same time, keeping them off public roads where they may be a danger to other road users. In addition, Zuckerman (1979) noted that former participants in a drug rehabilitation programme who took up parachute jumping after leaving the programme were able to experience a 'high' through a legal and relatively safe activity rather than in an illegal and personally harmful manner.

As Kaplan (1984: 55), pointed out,

> ... the delinquent activities that reflect subcultural values such as
> risk-taking might easily be substituted for in the minds of the youths

that share the culture. While delinquent activities might reflect the shared values of daring or toughness because of their association with the risk of apprehension by the police, so might other activities that in themselves are not illegal such as boxing, skydiving, or other behaviors that carry with them great risk of physical injury.

A range of other activities, apart from various types of sports, could be used to replace soccer hooligan behaviour. These should be non-harmful either to the individual concerned or to others. Conceivably, rewarding activities like illicit drug-taking, for example, could be used to replace hooligan activity but would of course be detrimental to the individual's health and would almost certainly cause different and more serious problems for society. Replacement activities of this type are therefore undesirable.

The abundance of soccer clubs in European countries and the relatively small distances between towns and cities, which allow travel to away matches, mean that, for the hooligan, the soccer environment provides a cheap and easily accessible means of managing hedonic tone. Finding an alternative that is as accessible and as cheap might not be easy. The choice of alternative activity will be governed by local patterns and traditions in leisure or individual patterns of lifestyle (Plant and Plant 1992). Risk sports, for example, are expensive, often requiring expensive equipment and sometimes considerable travel. Consequently, there is, for example, little point in introducing young offenders in detention centres to outdoor pursuit activities if these, or similar facilities, are not available to the offenders after their release. However, until other easily accessible and perhaps cheap activities can be found, or even provided, for soccer hooligans, especially hardcore superthugs, they are unlikely to cease their activities.

> It will be obvious that, although many of these intervention initiatives can be begun while the offender is still in custody, the crucial assistance is likely to be in the period of aftercare or rehabilitation of indefinite length following release which ends only with the establishment of a well-distributed pluralistic range of easily accessible rewarding activities which yield a high rate of reward i.e. a general improvement in the subjective quality of life on the straight.
>
> (Brown 1991b: 31)

Relapse crises are liable to occur in soccer hooligans when changes in the policy and style of hedonic tone management have proven ineffective. Recidivism is likely to be triggered by an assortment of cues. Unless the violent behaviour has been effectively extinguished, seeing television pictures about particular hooligan incidents, reading newspaper 'hype' about hooligan problems at forthcoming soccer tournaments or making renewed contact with former soccer hooligan mates, with the undoubted invitations to 'join the lads', may be enough to cause the hooligan to revert to violence. The eleventh and twelfth propositions of Brown's (1991b) model go beyond intervention to deal with clarifying the boundaries and distinctions of addictions and providing arguments for a value-free concept of addiction. These two propositions are only of indirect interest to a discussion of soccer hooliganism. However, it may be worth noting in passing that Brown argued strongly for a move away from moral and medical models of addiction to a value-free model for a better understanding of addictive behaviour. He said:

> It is time that the perception of addictions came out from under the dominance of moral and medical models which obscure our views of them and filter our perceptions of the wider context of phenomena within which they are embedded. Addictions are no more 'evil' or 'sick' as a particular case of the wider class of motivational monopolies and reward specialisms than tornados and hurricanes are 'evil' and 'sick' as a particular case of the wider spectrum of global weather systems involving winds.
>
> (Brown 1991b: 24–5)

Perhaps the media, who frequently 'dress up' their reports of soccer hooliganism using similar moral and medical terminology, should take note.

Why has hooliganism become associated with soccer and not some other sport or activity, and will it continue?

In England, most soccer hooligan fighting in the 1960s and early 1970s took place inside soccer grounds. This had little to do with soccer itself, beyond the fact that professional soccer provided an easily accessible (high availability and low cost) source of high arousal experiences. No other activity, sporting or otherwise, provided thrills in such abundance and was available in most of the large towns and cities in Britain and Europe on a frequent and regular basis. 'In those days the trouble was spontaneous and would usually erupt when one side scored a goal. Most fans get upset when a goal is scored against them, but for some the only remedy was to bust an opposing fan's nose. Of course, for many the football was incidental to the punch-up.' (Ward 1989: 9).

Later, in the late 1970s and the 1980s, the soccer clubs and the police began to adopt tactics that forced a change in hooligan violence. As a result of a number of measures (e.g. placing visiting groups in fenced pens under close police scrutiny), fighting inside the soccer grounds became more difficult and began to occur more frequently outside the stadia and often away from the ground altogether.

Further government measures, based largely on the safety recommendations of the Taylor Report on the Hillsborough disaster of 1989, have recently been taken. Perhaps the most significant of these measures is the abolition of soccer terraces. By the start of the 1994–5 season, all Premier League and First Division clubs must upgrade stadiums to all-seater facilities. The majority of clubs have already begun to comply, and standing terraces, such as the North Bank at Arsenal and the Stretford End at Manchester United, both notorious for hooligan violence in the past, have already been rebuilt into areas of seating. Fans, no longer able to participate in the terrace activities for so long a part of British soccer, are already complaining about lack of atmosphere at games. 'So, yes, of course it is sad; football crowds may yet be able to create a new environment that electrifies, but they will never be able to recreate the old one which required vast numbers and a context in which those numbers could form themselves into one huge reactive body' (Hornby 1992: 76).

Video monitoring systems have been installed at virtually all soccer grounds to allow police to monitor crowd movement and safety and to pin-point hooligan violence and direct police action should it be necessary. In addition, by the 'freeze framing' of particular shots of hooligan fighting, images of those involved can be enlarged and the chief troublemakers identified. Information about soccer hooligans is stored centrally in the data banks of computers in the National Criminal Intelligence Service and is available to assist police services in Britain and Europe. As described in Chapter 7, undercover police officers managed to infiltrate hooligan gangs and collect evidence that resulted in a number of top hooligans being prosecuted. However, not all government measures have been fully successful. Perimeter fencing around the playing area has been removed from many grounds and the identity card scheme that was pushed hard for a time by Prime Minister Thatcher never really materialized. Only the Luton Town club's membership scheme has worked successfully in terms of eradicating hooliganism. Their membership scheme allows entry to games for Luton fans only and excludes virtually all visiting fans (and hooligans).

It seems that with the implementation of these current measures, there is less and less likelihood of hooligan fighting taking place inside soccer grounds. To put it in a different way, the hooligan game has become unbalanced in favour of the police. The paratelic-negativistic 'fun' element of the hooligan game has been, to a large extent, removed. Apart from a few recent exceptions, when violence occurs it takes place well away from soccer grounds (e.g. Ward 1989: 181). Indeed, over the past two or three years the most serious soccer hooligan violence has been associated with England matches abroad. With the numbers of recent domestic hooligan incidents decreasing substantially, some politicians in England are starting to claim success in defeating the soccer hooligan problem. Could it possibly be that hooligan violence will be driven away from soccer altogether? As it becomes more and more difficult for the soccer hooligan to gain the desired quality of hedonic tone through self-fulfilling experiences within the soccer environment, it may be that they will eventually either stop or look elsewhere to other events as a venue for hooliganism.

Why do some soccer hooligans drop out or move on?

It may be that hooligans who drop out have simply become tired of, or apathetic about, an activity that was originally perceived as new and exciting, negativistic and deviant. Over the years, the make-up of individual soccer hooligan gangs has varied and the personnel changed or, as Cohen (1972: 200) put it, 'the original actors simply matured out'.

> I look back on my time on the terraces as an apprenticeship, part of the learning process, but just as children tend to grow out of asthma, so I grew out of my youthful behaviour. Some people don't however, and the use of weapons in football violence now by men in their late twenties and early thirties (some who are parents themselves) is a frightening fact of life.
>
> (Ward 1989: 182)

Cohen (1972) argued that the over-reaction of the authorities and the media to deviant behaviour acted as an amplifier of deviance, making the 'problem' behaviour much worse. He went on to suggest that, after a period of time, a kind of reverse process of deamplification of deviance might occur and that this was one reason for the demise of groups like the Mods and Rockers. It must be said that soccer hooliganism seems to have endured longer, and that the drop off has been less drastic than with some other deviant activities that were 'in vogue' at other times. However, it does appear that similar deamplification processes are at work in soccer hooliganism. At a certain point, the increasingly severe restrictions on soccer hooligans may become overbearing and some participants may drop out. 'The game was simply not worth it' (Cohen 1972: 202). At the same time, new recruits become less likely to join the group.

This is less likely to be true for the addicted hooligans who find it extremely difficult, or refuse, to give up hooligan fighting and who often stay involved until their late twenties or even early thirties. It may be for them that other sporting events, such as cricket, rugby league or rugby union, may offer new possibilities. Over the past six years or so, there have been reports of 'soccer hooligan-type' violence occurring in other sports contexts. For example, during England's cricket tour to Australia in 1986–7, England were victorious in the final of a one-day cricket competition known as the Benson and Hedges Challenge. Mosey (1987: 224) wrote: 'It was unfortunate that victory in the final of the Challenge should be marred by post-match violence by drunken hooligans, many of them waving Union Jacks and some carrying knives. This led to 25 arrests and a call from the police for sales of liquor at cricket matches to be either banned, or at least limited.'

Other non-sporting locations have also been venues for soccer hooligan-type violence, including drunken violence in holiday resorts and so-called 'rural rioting' by 'lager louts'. Resorts in the Costa Brava area of Spain are patrolled by riot police, whose task is to move in and break up trouble when it occurs. Trouble occurs regularly during the summer when the resorts have thousands of young visitors. Not all the hooligans are English but much of what happens is soccer hooliganism, albeit in a different context. The incident described below by Hooper (1988) did have a soccer connection, but the majority do not.

> By the time we get to Jimmy's Fun Bar, the brawlers have fled and the waitresses are clearing the broken glass from the terrace. One of them has blood flowing down her legs. A waiter tells me it was a fight between Liverpool and Juventus supporters. Minutes later, speaking to the police he denies all knowledge of the cause.

'Lager louts', as they have been dubbed in the press, generally have prosperous occupations with good career prospects and family backgrounds. At weekends they engage in pub-fighting and vandalism (e.g. Smith and Logan 1988). In their article, Smith and Logan provided a number of quotes from active lager louts. The contents of these quotes are very similar to example quotes given earlier in this book from soccer hooligans. They contain the familiar remarks about being bored and being driven to drink and fighting to get a 'buzz' out of life. Typical of the lager louts is a twenty-year-old who is married with a wife and baby son and has his own successful taxi business. He is reported as saying, 'I just need three or four pints and I flip. When I go out on a Friday and Saturday night I'm hoping for a punch-up. It's like having a split personality' (Smith and Logan 1988: 7). Sometimes lager louts choose a small rural town and go there in numbers. They know that the police will be caught off-guard without sufficient resources in the area and the hooligans can engage in 'rural rioting', at least for a time, without hindrance. Alternatively, there are some regular venues where drunken violence occurs every Friday or Saturday night. One example is Ilkeston, a small market town in Derbyshire with a population of 33,000, but here, because of the regularity of the fighting, the Derbyshire police are usually prepared for trouble. Reports from the police confirm the view that 'unemployment is not the problem – the drinkers are well dressed and have enough money to pour up to 10 pints of beer down their necks' (Lonsdale 1991: 31).

Apart from the context, there would seem to be little difference in the motivation behind the violence and vandalism engaged in by lager louts, holiday hooligans and soccer hooligans. Whether this is just another form of hooliganism that has been present in Britain for years (Pearson 1983) or whether the apparent increase in such incidents in recent years is another case of moral panic (Cohen 1972) is open to debate. The important point is, however, that as hooligan behaviour in and around soccer becomes increasingly restricted, soccer hooligans may move their activities to different venues, sporting or otherwise. While the soccer clubs and authorities would be pleased with this change, the police may not see the implications of such a change in such a positive light. For them, soccer hooliganism has been a problem for about thirty years, but because it has been linked with soccer matches it has been relatively easy to contain. Over time, the police have learned how to limit it as much as possible. If hooligans move away from soccer to other activities and locations that are diverse and sometimes chosen at random, there is a likelihood of a real problem developing, with much more serious violence and fighting, which would be much more difficult to limit. Winning the battle against hooliganism in the soccer context may simply open a much bigger 'can of worms' elsewhere.

Closing comments

Although there are other forms of hooliganism, hooliganism associated with professional soccer is the form that has maintained a lead position in the media attention since the mid-1960s. Other types, such as 'steaming' on the London underground or at the Notting Hill festival in London, where gangs of youths run through a crowd or train carriage, grabbing valuable articles like handbags and radios and making off with them, briefly make the headlines, but not for long.

In spite of attempts by some academics to argue otherwise (Dunning *et al.* 1982), soccer hooliganism in its contemporary form is, generally speaking, a relatively new form of hooliganism. According to Pearson (1983), hooliganism has been a feature of British society for quite some time. Indeed, there is evidence of a whole host of activities that have a long history and serve the same function in other societies that hooliganism (or soccer hooliganism) does in English or Western European societies. The American anthropologist Foster (1988) has argued, providing examples from history and various cultures around the world, that what she has termed 'culturally triggered reversals' are required for the viability and maintenance of stability within a particular culture. If she is correct, it would seem that, for all the apparent disorder and unrest that soccer hooliganism causes, it may well serve an important stabilizing function for society in general.

Apter (1992) followed a similar line of reasoning with regard to arousal-seeking and risk-taking behaviour, which he claimed played an important role in biological, cultural and personal evolution. He also contended that the opportunities for young people to engage in arousal-seeking behaviour in contemporary society are diminishing (see also Elias and Dunning 1970). As Western society attempts to build more stable and secure communities and the possibilities, for example, to fight in wars or undertake pioneering geographical exploration become increasingly diminished, young people will continue to come up with new and perhaps more extreme ways to take risks, some of which may be decidedly antisocial in nature. It may not be just coincidental that rioting, sometimes without any apparent reason, has broken out in recent years in normally quiet and conservative cities in Britain, such as Oxford and Cardiff in 1991.

If opportunities for arousal seeking are decreasing but arousal seeking serves an important function in society, then it may be that some forms of deviant behaviour are best left alone. For instance, perhaps instead of clamping down on soccer hooligan violence, the authorities should not only leave it alone, but actually encourage it. After the soccer match, the players could leave the pitch and fans only interested in the game could leave the stadium. Hooligans could then be left to fight it out in a kind of soccer hooligan 'high noon' or 'roller derby', involving violence between consenting adults! All of this would take place within the confined area of the stadium and innocent members of the public and the police force would remain uninvolved and uninjured. In addition, the press and other media could be banned from reporting the fighting (Cohen 1972). This, of course, would rob soccer hooliganism of much of its excitement and it has to be wondered how long soccer hooliganism would continue if the authorities attempted such a policy.

A more positive approach from the authorities would be to encourage people to take part in dangerous, risk-taking activities, preferably those that are not harmful to others. Perhaps the streets of Leeds and Manchester could be blocked off and people could be allowed to 'run before the bulls' as they do Pamplona in Spain; perhaps London's bridges or the Telecom Tower could be used for bungie jumping and tall buildings for mountaineering; perhaps Donnington or Silverstone race tracks should have periods of free access for young people to race cars or motor bikes against each other. If people, especially young people, in sufficient numbers could have access to other forms of risk taking, their need to experience high arousal would be catered for in a more socially acceptable, non-damaging way.

In the longer term, education is crucial to this process. Through education, in the broadest sense of the word, children and young people need to learn how to experience, for example, high arousal through curiosity and empathy, without having to resort to basic or primitive strategies through anger and violence, which result in vandalism, delinquency or soccer hooliganism. By the time the young person reaches adulthood, a repertoire of habits, skills and knowledge should have been built up which allows the person to experience a wide range of emotions and deal with life's difficulties in a mature way (Apter and Kerr 1991: 170).

Finally, by way of comparison with the activities of gangs in major American cities, soccer hooliganism is, perhaps, a rather benign form of hooliganism. The use of high-powered automatic guns in American gang shootings means that there is always a possibility that a real bloodbath will occur. American gang warfare involves a much more brutal and malevolent form of violence, as yet unknown in the context of soccer hooliganism. Europe may have the problem of soccer hooliganism, but America's hooligan problem is 'a different ball game'.

Attempting to unravel the motivation behind much of human behaviour can sometimes be a perplexing task. Soccer hooliganism, the aspect of human behaviour under discussion in this book, is no less complex than any other form of paradoxical human behaviour. However, by the use of reversal theory concepts perhaps an improved understanding of the motivational processes behind soccer hooligan behaviour can be achieved.

References

Apter, M. J. (1989). *Reversal Theory: Motivation, Emotion and Personality*. London: Routledge.

Apter, M. J. (1991). 'A structural phenomenology of play', in J. H. Kerr and M. J. Apter (eds) *Adult Play: a Reversal Theory Approach*. Amsterdam: Swets and Zeitlinger, pp. 163–76.

Apter, M. J. (1992). *The Dangerous Edge*. New York: Free Press.

Apter, M. J. and Kerr, J. H. (1991). 'The nature, function and value of play', in J. H. Kerr and M. J. Apter (eds) *Adult Play: a Reversal Theory Approach*. Amsterdam: Swets and Zeitlinger, pp. 163–76.

Bowers, A. J. (1988). 'Telic dominance and delinquency in adolescent boys', in M. J. Apter, J. H. Kerr and M. P. Cowles (eds) *Progress in Reversal Theory*. Amsterdam: North-Holland Elsevier, pp. 191–211.

Brown, R. I. F. (1988). 'Reversal theory and subjective experience in the explanation of addiction and relapse', in M. J. Apter, J. H. Kerr and M. P. Cowles (eds) *Progress in Reversal Theory*. Amsterdam: North-Holland, pp. 191–211.

Brown, R. I. F. (1991a). 'Gaming, gambling and other addictive play', in J. H. Kerr and M. J. Apter (eds) *Adult Play: a Reversal Theory Approach*. Amsterdam: Swets and Zeitlinger, pp. 101–18.

Brown, R. I. F. (1991b). 'Mood management, self states as goals and addiction models of criminal behaviour'. Paper presented at the British Psychological Society Division of Criminal and Legal Psychology and Department of Psychology, Rampton Hospital Conference, Addicted to Crime, Nottingham, March.

Buford, B. (1991). *Among the Thugs*. London: Secker and Warburg.

Canter, D., Comber, M. and Uzzell, D. L. (1989). *Football in Its Place*. London and New York: Routledge.

Cohen, S. (1972). *Folk Devils and Moral Panics*. Oxford: Blackwell.

Davies, D. (1985). 'Affluent fans lead fighting'. *The Observer*, 6 June.

Dunning, E., Maguire, J. A., Murphy, P. J. and Williams, J. M. (1982). The social roots of football hooliganism. *Leisure Studies*, 2, 139–56.

Dunning, E., Murphy, P. J. and Williams, J. (1986). 'Spectator violence at football matches: Towards a sociological explanation'. *British Journal of Sociology*, 37(2), 221–44.

Elias, N. and Dunning, E. (1970). 'The quest for excitement in unexciting societies', in G. Luschen (ed.) *A Cross-cultural Analysis of Sports and Games*. Champaign, IL: Stipes, pp. 31–51.

Faster, M. L. (1988). 'Cultural triggering of psychological reversals' in M. J. Apter, J. H. Kerr and M. P. Cowles (eds) *Progress In Reversal Theory*. Amsterdam: Elsevier, pp. 63–75.

Harrington, J. A. (1968). *Soccer Hooliganism*. Bristol: John Wright and Sons.

Hooper, J. (1988). 'When fun turns to violence'. *Guardian*, 16 August.

Hornby, N. (1992). *Fever Pitch*. London: Victor Gollancz.

Hull, J. G. and Bond, R. D. (1986). 'Social and behavioral consequences of alcohol consumption and expectancy: a meta-analysis'. *Psychological Bulletin*, 99, 347–60.

Jones, R. (1981). 'Reversals, delinquency and fun'. *European Journal of Humanistic Psychology*, 9(5), 237–40.

Kaplan, H. B. (1984). *Patterns of Juvenile Delinquency*. London: Sage.

Keel, P. (1987). 'Terraces of terror'. *Guardian*, 9 May, 19.

Kerr, J. H. (1988). 'Soccer hooliganism and the search for excitement', in M. J. Apter, J. H. Kerr and M. P. Cowles (eds) *Progress in Reversal Theory*. Amsterdam: Elsevier North-Holland, pp. 191–211.

Klapp, O. E. (1986). *Overload and Boredom*. New York: Greenwood Press.

Lonsdale, S. (1991). 'Crime: days of beer and bruises'. *The Observer Magazine*, 17 February, 31.

Marsh, P. (1978). *Aggro: the Illusion of Violence*. London: Dent.

Mosey, D. (1987). *Botham*. London: Sphere Books.

Murgatroyd, S. and Apter, M. J. (1986). 'A structural phenomenological approach to eclectic psychotherapy', in J. Norcross (ed.) *Handbook of Eclectic Psychotherapy*. New York: Brunner/Mazel, pp. 260–80.

Pearson, G. (1983). *A History of Respectable Fears*. London: Macmillan.

Plant, M. and Plant, M. (1992). *Risk-takers: Alcohol, Drugs, Sex and Youth*. London: Routledge.

Reade, E. (1984) 'Vandalism: is household movement a substitute for social control?' in C. Levy-Leboyer (ed.) *Vandalism: Behaviour and Motivations*. Amsterdam: North-Holland, pp. 133–48.

Robins, D. (1984). *We Hate Humans*. Harmondsworth: Penguin.

Smith, A. and Logan, C. (1988). 'Make the lager louts pay, courts ordered'. *Sunday Express*, 18 September, 7.

Taylor, E. (1984). 'I was a soccer hooligan – Class of 64'. *Guardian*, 28 March.

Taylor, I. R. (1971). 'Soccer conciousness and soccer hooliganism', in S. Cohen (ed.) *Images of Deviance*. Harmondsworth: Penguin, pp. 134–64.

Taylor, I. (1976). 'Spectator violence around football: the rise and fall of the "Working Class Weekend"'. *Research Papers in Physical Education*, 4(1), 4–9.

Taylor, I. (1987). 'Putting the boot into working class sport: British soccer after Bradford and Brussels'. *Sociology of Sport Journal*, 4, 171–91.

Thayer, R. E. (1989). *The Biopsychology of Mood and Arousal*. Oxford: University of Oxford Press.

Thompson, T. (1988). 'Joyride? You mean deathride'. *The Observer*, 35.

Trivizas, E. (1980). 'Offences and offenders in football crowd disorders'. *British Journal of Criminology*, 20(3), 276–88.

Van der Molen, P. P. (1985). 'Learning, self-actualization and psychotherapy', in M. J. Apter, D. Fontana and S. Murgatroyd (eds) *Reversal Theory: Applications and Developments*. New York: Lawrence Erlbaum, pp. 103–116.

Van der Molen, P. P. (1986). 'Reversal, learning and psychotherapy'. *British Journal of Guidance and Counselling*, 14(2), 125–39.

Walter, A. J. (1978). *Sent Away: a Study of Young Offenders in Care*. Hampshire: Saxon House.

Ward, C. (1989). *Steaming in*. London: Simon and Schuster.

Williams, J., Dunning, E. and Murphy, P. (1984). *Hooligans Abroad*. London: Routledge and Kegan Paul.

Zuckerman, M. (1979). *Sensation Seeking: Beyond the Optimal Level of Arousal*. Hillsdale, NJ: L. Erlbaum.

AUTHOR INDEX

SUBJECT INDEX

YOUTH AND INEQUALITY

Inge Bates and George Riseborough

This book consists of a unique and fascinating collection of qualitative and ethno-graphic studies of differing groups of young people. It examines inequality in all its complexity in the lived experience of youth and shows the continued pervasive influence of class and gender. The groups studied range from young women in private education to youth training 'lads' and gives vivid and insightful accounts of their social existence. Their diverse experiences are explored in the context of family, education, training, work and politics. The contributors consider for exam-ple, family and educational processes, social divisions and control, identities and opportunities, 'enterprise' careers and cultural resistance in the context of late/post modern transitions. *Youth and Inequality* is essential reading for students and researchers in the social sciences, education and cultural studies and will be of interest to all those professionally engaged with young people.

Contents
Introduction – A job which is 'right for me'? Social class, gender and individualization – Learning a living or living a learning? an ethnography of BTEC National Diploma students – 'When I have my own studio . . .' the making and shaping of 'designer' careers – Running, plodding and falling: the practice and politics of youth enter-prise – A yuppie generation? Political and cultural options for A-level students – Gaining the edge: girls at a private school – becoming privileged: the role of family processes – 'GBH – The Gobbo Barmy Harmy': one day in the life of 'the YTS boys' – Career trajectories and the mirage of increased social mobility – Index.

Contributors
Patricia Allatt, Inge Bates, Rob MacDonald, John Quicke, George Riseborough, Ken Roberts, Debra Roker.

272pp   0 335 15695 9 (Paperback)

MOTHERHOOD AND MODERNITY
AN INVESTIGATION INTO THE RATIONAL DIMENSION OF MOTHERING

Christine Everingham

This book takes a central topic in women's studies and sociology of the family and presents an innovative analysis linking motherhood to broader sociological debates on modernity, rationality and individuation. It has many strengths, including a well handled mix of theoretical and ethnographic material, a focused review of contemporary discussions of rationality and the self, an excellent review of the literature on mothering and morality, and perhaps most importantly, an insightful and illuminating central hypothesis which will promote lively debate.

Current models of mothering are based on the assumption that infants have biologically determined 'needs' that mothers learn to recognize and meet in socially approved ways. Christine Everingham develops an alternative model of nurturing that locates mothers as subjects, actively constructing the perspective of their child while asserting their own needs and interests in a particular socio-cultural context. This powerful book extends contemporary scholarly debates on mothering and modernity and is a valuable resource for teaching in women's studies and sociology.

Contents
Part one: The mother as subject – Mothering and feminist theory – Mothering and morality – The self in social theory. Part two: The study – The study – Maternal attitudes – Taking the attitude of the child – Maternal attitudes and maternal-infant conflict. Part three: Conclusion – The politics of the particular and the generalized 'other' – Bibliography – Index.

168p   0 335 19195 9 (Paperback)   0 335 19196 7 (Hardback)

TEXTUALITY AND TECTONICS
TROUBLING SOCIAL AND PSYCHOLOGICAL SCIENCE

Beryl C. Curt

In the market place of ideas, Social Science, plc, is in deep trouble! Exposed for decades to a 'climate of problematization', its foundational structures and technological practices – indeed the very project of a science of the social – have been eroded by critical, post-structural, social constructionist and postmodern analyses.

Textuality and Tectonics seeks neither to gloat upon this threatened bankruptcy, nor to peddle false hopes of a 'quick fix' restructuring under new management. Instead it concentrates upon and argues out the new prospects, alternative projects and liberated commitments opened up by the 'climate of problematization' itself. It takes on this task seriously but far from sombrely, celebrating the chance 'to boldly go' on a diversity of new enterprises, in a narrative rich in lively asides and opportunities for reflection. The result is a concerned 'critical polytextualism' which stresses the possibilities for new forms of transdisciplinary analytic craft and illustrates their use in practice.

Textuality and Tectonics will be a key text for students and scholars looking for new conceptual directions and alternative craft-skills for empirical enquiry at a time when 'social science' is 'going critical'. It will be invaluable not just for those working in its conventional disciplines (including anthropology, psychology and sociology) but for those in newer fields such as cultural and communication studies.

Contents
Having words with the reader – Textuality – Tectonics – Counterpoint – Crafty dodges – the question and questioning of methods – Topologies of representation – Topologies of understanding – Topologies of conduct – Inconclusion – Glossary – References – Index.

272pp   0 335 19063 4 (Paperback)   0 335 19064 2 (Hardback)